Reinventing Print

Cover:
A double page spread from the pocket-sized Caslon & Co type specimen book of 1832 showing 'forty-five line *Antique* compressed' – a style that other foundries called *Egyptian*. The choice of the word 'DIE' was the compositor's response to the foreboding appearance of the heavy slab serif – that and the lack of space with which to display it. A dark, often self-mocking humour is a regular feature within the printer's work and culture.

BLOOMSBURY VISUAL ARTS
Bloomsbury Publishing Plc
50 Bedford Square, London, WC1B 3DP, UK

BLOOMSBURY, BLOOMSBURY VISUAL ARTS and the Diana logo are trademarks of Bloomsbury Publishing Plc

Cover design: Louise Dugdale
Book design: David Jury

A catalogue record for this book is available from the British Library.

Library of Congress Cataloging-in-Publication Data
Names: Jury, David, author.
Title: Reinventing print : technology and craft in typography / David Jury.
Description: London ; New York : Bloomsbury Visual Arts, 2017. | Includes
  bibliographical references and index.
Identifiers: LCCN 2017006519| ISBN 9781474262699 (paperback : alk. paper) |
  ISBN 9781474262705 (ePDF) | ISBN 9781474262712 (epub)
Subjects: LCSH: Graphic design (Typography) | Graphic design
  (Typography)–Data processing. | Printing. | Digital printing. | Type and
  type-founding–Digital techniques. | Desktop publishing. | Electronic
  publishing. | Graphic arts–History–20th century. | Design–History–20th
  century. | Art and technology–History–20th century.
Classification: LCC Z246 .J87 2017 | DDC 686.2/2–dc23 LC record available at
https://lccn.loc.gov/2017006519

ISBN:
PB: 978-1-4742-6269-9
ePDF: 978-1-4742-6270-5
eBook: 978-1-4742-6271-2

Printed and bound in India

To find out more about our authors and books visit www.bloomsbury.com.

David Jury

Reinventing Print: Technology and Craft in Typography

BLOOMSBURY VISUAL ARTS
LONDON · NEW YORK · OXFORD · NEW DELHI · SYDNEY

Contents

Previous page:
William H Bradley, printed woodcut, detail from the cover of *The American Chapbook*, issue number one, published by the American Type Founders Company, (ATF) 1904.

Bradley's illustration depicts an 18th-century street vendor selling chapbooks – small, folded, unbound booklets, crudely printed, which sold for a penny. Bookshops existed but their stock was expensive – even newspapers were beyond the means of most people, so the chapbook was the sole reading material in many family homes.

Below:
Libreria book shop, which opened in London 2016. The concept of the small bookshop is attracting a new generation of proprietors or 'entrepreneurs'. In the spirit of famous bookshops, such as Shakespeare and Company in Paris (see page 78) and City Lights in San Francisco, Libreria is cultivating itself as a community hub and even owns a printing press with which it intends to publish limited edition books.

The curved yellow shelving, designed by students from Central St Martin's School of Art, lends a free-spirited, cheerfully bohemian aura.

Opposite page:
Caffè Nero, free-standing printed notice, 2016, using 'rough-hewn' hand-drawn lettering that incorporates low-tech photocopier process. The 'dressed-down' appearance is calculated to entice customers to partake in a survey and the possibility of winning, ironically that icon of sophistication, an iPad.

Introduction

Digital technology and printed media

For a brief period, screen-based digital technology seemed destined to supplant all other text-carrying media. Digital technology is, after all, more mobile, searchable, editable and sharable, so what could possibly stop it eliminating print? Just as the rise and influence of print culture is linked with the establishment of modern industrial society, so the demise of print was being linked with the decline of Modernism as a 'new media' – a digital revolution no less – rose to dominate every aspect of contemporary life. Since the mid-1990s, the Internet has had an immense impact on culture, commerce, and technology, including the rise of near-instant communication by electronic mail, instant messaging, two-way interactive video calls, and, of course, the World Wide Web with its discussion forums, blogs, social networking, and online shopping sites. In that process, paper-based media underwent a rigorous examination, the result being that some of its most heroic, prestigious and apparently indispensable achievements (for example, the dictionary, thesaurus, encyclopaedia, directories) were found to be the most vulnerable.

Graphic communication – printed ink on paper – has, in fact, been threatened with imminent obsolescence on many occasions. However, its demise was always postponed because technology could not, finally, deliver what the imagination had concocted. However, with the arrival of the desktop computer in 1984 everything changed and, together with the invention of the Internet in 1989, a communications revolution was heralded and was, without doubt, a genuine and very practical threat to print.

Yet today, almost thirty years later, the sight of newspaper vendors has not diminished and the number of magazines being published has not only grown enormously, their design and contents has become more diverse than ever. The number of independent bookshops has fallen, but this has not been due to digital technology replacing the printed book, indeed, the number of books being published continues to grow, but rather, competition from on-line 'stores'. In response, a new generation of bookshops have begun to appear, offering bright esoteric spaces with their own distinctive choice of books. Many have cultivated themselves as a community hub: a strategy pioneered by the famous Shakespeare and Company bookshop, Paris, since 1922 (page 78) and still going strong today. Libreria, a book-shop recently opened in London is typical of such new enterprises, and even has

Below:
Printing room of the world's oldest and most influential Jewish newspaper, the London-based *Jewish Chronicle* which was founded in 1841.

Below right:
Studio at Woodcote Publications, 1974, UK. The graphic designer required a broad range of tools, equipment and materials prior to digital technology and so the working space tended to be more cluttered than today (see opposite page). Work was done on drawing tables which had parallel motion – a pulley system that enabled a fixed transparent ruler to be slid up and down the table. The large box-like object to the left in the background is a Grant Projector (see page 101). Note the telephone in the foreground.

its own letterpress printing press offering typography and printing classes and provides support for small independent publishing ventures.

The form of the book and its component parts survives because it remains the most effective, efficient and attractive 'interface' ever conceived. First devised between the 2nd and 4th centuries, the means of printing multiple copies was invented some 670 years ago, since when its essential form has remained indisputable. Until, that is, the change from mechanical and analogue electronic technology to digital electronics during the latter decades of the 20th century. The death of print was announced with uncommon speed – a story merrily reported more often than not by the print media itself – this was, after all, an excellent story and one that helped to sell millions of newspapers, magazines and books.

Apparently facing catastrophe, publishers were impelled to respond. They did this (with the aid of typographers, graphic designers, printers, photographers, illustrators etc) by reinventing print as an infinitely more flexible, malleable and inventive medium than its digital rival. In achieving this, emphasis was, ironically, focused once more on those same aspects of printed media that had previously been described as the reasons for its inevitable demise: its physical presence – mass, weight and volume In other words, an object to be touched, held, opened and which later required a place on a table or a shelf – all had suddenly become something to savour. The making of this object, even a modest paperback, embodied sufficient largesse to bestow a warmth that the digital screen can not achieve. And it is the making in which craft and creative endeavour – those very elements that add that vital generosity of spirit – lie.

'Craft' concerns the ability to control, certainly tools and materials. For designers of information to be received on variously sized digital screens control was an 'indulgence' to be relinquished in return for an active part in the development of a new and extraordinary means of communication. This lack control became, briefly, a means of expression, a statement by which a new generation of typographers could

Below:
Lundgren+Lindqvist design studio, Gothenburg, Sweden, 2016.

Initially, when digital technology was developing quickly, it became a major preoccupation for designers. Indeed, the appearance of studio computers, their power and *au courant* status, came to represent a company's commitment to innovation and technical prowess as well as the efficiencies it promised.

Today, it is more likely that the design studio will reflect very different social, cultural and ecological values (books, fresh fruit, green transport) ahead of technology. The poster on the wall is by Wim Crouwel (see page 108).

distance itself from the past. With so little control, knowledge of how to make a text readable no longer seemed to hold any value. Until, that is, it was realised that the medium of paper and ink was not, after all, about to expire.

Digital technology and typography

In the time between the appearance of the Apple MacIntosh and the establishment of the Internet there existed an unprecedented feeling of typographic euphoria. For a relatively small investment in hardware and software, typographers were able to harness the industry's type technology direct from their own desktops. For a few years this capability was liberating – no longer requiring the services of a phototypesetter or printer's compositor – and the result was an rush of intensive typographic invention.

There was also an immediate reordering of the broader typographic landscape as the historic behemoths (such as Monotype, Berthold and Linotype-Hell) were forced to slim down, consolidate or seek out niches in a market that they had previously monopolized. In their place emerged software firms (most significantly Adobe) who arrived at type almost inadvertently through the development of desktop publishing technology. But it was the rise of independent type designers such as Zuzana Licko who seized the imagination *and* the design initiative.

It is the ambitions and alliances of the typographer and graphic designer which are the main preoccupation of this book. As outlined above, the past thirty years have been a torrid time: the sudden rise, popularity and integration of the Internet so emphatically into our social and commercial fabric caused graphic designers to question the future nature of their profession. The very word 'graphic' (meaning 'print') suddenly felt antiquated and inhibiting, the sense of foreboding given emphasis by the establishment of new degree courses solely in digital and website design. Perhaps aware of their profession's own origins many were fearful that digital technology was going to do to graphic design what the graphic designer had done

to the printer some 100 years previously (essentially, steal control of print away from the printer). Today, the prospectuses of the remaining website design courses talk less about the exciting potential of digital technology and more about the 'integrated' structure of the course, emphasising links to graphic design, advertising, marketing and time-based media courses within the institution. In other words, digital media has become one of the many integrated means of communication required by the commercial sector.

Nevertheless, digital technology has caused both typographer and graphic designer to re-evaluate the relatively short history of their professions and their contribution to cultural life and commercial effectiveness. Early in the 20th century the allure of print was its democratic potential. At the beginning of the 21st century that distinction had moved firmly to the Internet. And yet, a mere decade later, the number of books and magazines being published in the wake of the digital revolution continues to grow and, perhaps more important, the breadth of what is on offer is greater than ever. This rediscovery of print has been reflected in the phenomenal growth in specialist book fairs for independent artist/designer/printer-publishers and is testament to the fascination for craft and craftsmanship in today's post-digital age. The New York Book Fair, organised by Printed Matter, boasts 36,000 visitors during its annual four-day event. Meanwhile, the Frankfurt Book Fair, the world's largest trade fair for books, had more than seven thousand exhibitors and more than 278,000 visitors during five days in 2016. At such gatherings – and there are multifarious print and publishing fairs held in every major city around the world, London currently has at least five – it is difficult to imagine that print has *ever* been more influential, or more popular and vibrant than it is today.

If this is true, could print ever have been accurately described as being in decline? Digital technology is no longer the daring new technology of boundless possibilities, but instead, something to which we have grown accustomed and its possibilities understood. Now seems an appropriate moment to step back and reflect on the current role and profession of the typographer, graphic designer, printer and publisher, and the saga of paper and/or pixels.

Below and below right:
Albert Robida, illustration and cover from *Le Vingtième Siècle.* written and illustrated by Robida, Paris 1890.

This and similar books by Robida drew comparison with Jules Verne. But, unlike Verne, Robida proposed inventions that were part of everyday life and imagined the social developments that arose from them, often accurately: social advancement of women, mass tourism, pollution, communication etc. For example, the 'téléphonoscope' (below) is imagined as a flat-screen display that delivers twenty-four hour news as well as theatrical events, educational courses, and business teleconferences.

Opposite page, top:
An 'e-reader' as imagined in the pages of the American magazine, *Everyday Science and Mechanics*, April 1935. *(Illustrator not credited.)*

Opposite page, bottom:
Telephone and telegraph wires over Broadway, 1890. 'Wires snapped on a regular basis [...] thrashing about, spraying sparks in all directions.' From *Book of Old New York*, Henry C Brown, 1913.

Preamble

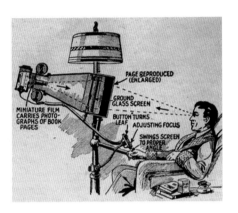

Nineteenth century perceptions of technology

For the city dweller, communications and media technologies that came to fruition in the late 19th and early 20th centuries already constituted an embryonic 'world wide web'. High-speed transport links enabled mechanised distribution systems whilst the telegraph and then the telephone and radio were all in place by the 1920s. The vision of the 'global village', proclaimed by Marshall McLuhan some forty years later, was already under construction.[1]

'Technological miracles' were being reported in the press on an almost daily basis in the lead-up to 1900. The perceived inevitability of technological progress meant not only that expectations were on a constant high, but also a sense of nonchalance, even tedium crept into the reporting: '...the times in which we live may well be called the "age of invention". Never before, it would seem, have men so ardently studied the secrets of nature and turned the knowledge thus acquired to practical account. We have become so accustomed to hearing of new inventions that nowadays they hardly surprise us.'[2]

But acceptance of technology did not come without reservations. In fact, and especially in the first half of the 19th century, 'change' had been considered by some to be dangerous; it suggested a dissatisfaction with the status quo and an acceptance of the 'unknown'. As a result, religious and sociopolitical organisations sought to link, for example, steam technology, with predictions of apocalyptic catastrophe by arguing that it upset the essential balance of the planet. The fear was that natural constituent forces might, in some way, be irreparably damaged by new-found 'unnatural' power sources. Put starkly, there was a simple choice: technology or religion; progress or redemption. Working conditions within factories and on huge building projects – for example, digging tunnels for underground steam trains – were compared to Biblical descriptions of hell. There was a genuine sense that humanity was overreaching itself and heading toward an indefinable disaster.

At the very zenith of this industrial and technological maelstrom John Ruskin, art critic and social reformer, called for a return to a more human-orientated approach to social progress, focusing on the aspirations and creative potential of the individual. In his prodigious writings Ruskin emphasised the connections between art, nature and society and was vehemently critical of technologies being applied to the mass production of goods. Ruskin's criticisms of 'modern' life, especially

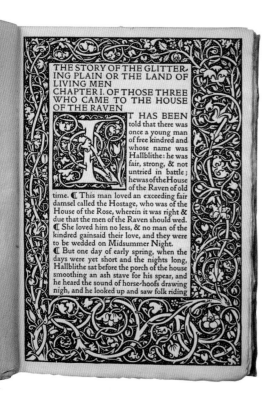

Above:
William Morris, *The Story of the Glittering Plain*, London, 1891. This was Morris's first book to be printed by his own Kelmscott Press.

The heavy, handmade papers and cover boards, the dense black ink and large strong type are all a conscious contrast with the ubiquitous and more flamboyant Art Nouveau style so popular in everyday printed material as well as the distinguished 'fine' or 'deluxe' printing as represented by Octave Uzanne and Oscar Wilde (opposite page).

concerning the loss of individual skills to mechanization and resultant loss of pride or personal responsibility, resonated across Victorian society. William Morris, designer, writer, socialist and a key supporter of Ruskin's ideals explained, 'Nothing should be made by man's labour which is not worth making, or which must be made by labour degrading to the maker.'[3] The Arts and Crafts Exhibition Society was set up in 1887 and similar organisations across North America and Europe adapted Arts and Crafts philosophy according to their own needs.

However, by the final decade of the 19th century, criticism of technology was dissipating. Not only had the predicted apocalypse not arrived, but living standards were rising and, with the aid of new technologies, manufacturing was bringing down the cost of household goods. In comparison, the handmade chair or table – once the only available option – was now expensive, indeed 'handmade' increasingly meant 'luxury'. Morris himself had huge difficulties coming to terms with the fact that he was, in his own words, 'ministering to the swinish rich'[4] at a time when, intellectually at least, he was preoccupied with the concerns of the poor.

Consequently, the last decade of the 19th century was one of contrasts regarding attitudes to technology. New sources of power, first steam but then more importantly electricity, had matured and were already demonstrating new-found advantages in a myriad of ways, including communication. The radicalism of Victorian ambition was coming to fruition, even transcended, as a new wave of young artists and designers rebuked Ruskin and Morris's adherence to the glories of the past and, instead, embraced the concept of change that technology promised. There was a genuine sense of being on the threshold of a new and golden age; a technological Utopia that must be grasped. 'We are all standing at the open door of a great century,' reported the *British Workman* journal in 1897, a year after Morris's death. It was not so much that there were better times to come, but that such times were inevitable.

It was Thomas Edison who best captured the public's imagination. Having registered more than a thousand patents he was the embodiment of the ingenious inventor intent on single-handedly changing the world. Authors of the 19th century repeatedly investigated the theme of science and its moral predicaments, one of the earliest and famous being Mary Shelly's *Frankenstein* in 1812. Others include *The Los Amigos Fiasco* (1892) in which Arthur Conan Doyle 'improved' the electric chair so that the victim is, inadvertently, supercharged with electricity and appears to be made immortal. H G Wells created a number of lone inventors: Griffin, who masters invisibility in *The Invisible Man* (1897), Cavor, who discovers an antigravity material in *First Men in the Moon* (1901), the unnamed inventor of *The Time Machine* (1895) and, most sinister of all, Dr Moreau who experiments in turning animals into humans in *The Island of Doctor Moreau* (1896). In every case electric power played a key role. Not surprising then that electricity was described as the 'new elixir of life'.[5]

In the final decade of the 19th century the popular press was awash with predictions and prophesies of what technology would provide during the next hundred years. The French were particularly keen on futuristic musing and the most influential, particularly concerning the future of printing, was Octave Uzanne's extended article 'La Fin des Livres' ('The End of Books'). It was published in the

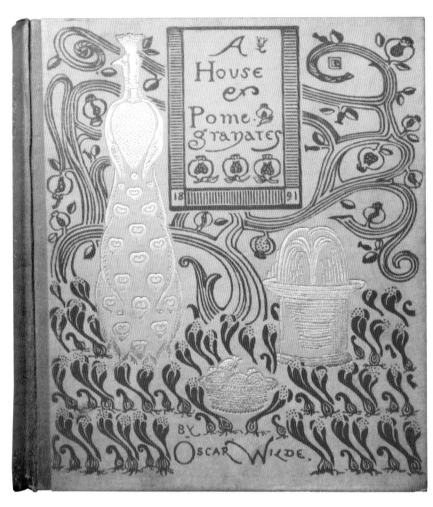

Above left:

Paul Avril, cover of *L'éventail* ('The Fan') a book written by Octave Uzanne, Paris, 1882.

This was Uzanne's first and most famous book, which he admitted was 'in no way a work of powerful wisdom and erudition', but simply the first of an intended series of 'little books for the boudoir'.

To place such extravagant production at the service of such a frivolous subject was wholly typical of the Art Nouveau. It was this attitude: 'art for art's sake' (rather than seeking a higher moral purpose) that so dramatically distinguished it from the deeply moral stance engaged by the Arts and Crafts movement.

Above right:

Charles Ricketts, cover design for Oscar Wilde's book of fairy tales, *The House of Pomegranates*, London, 1891, the same year that Morris published his first Kelmscott Press book (opposite page). When Morris reprinted *The Story of the Glittering Plain* (opposite page) in 1894, he commissioned Ricketts to provide the illustrations.

American *Scribner's Magazine* in 1894.[6] Uzanne was a writer, editor, publisher of visually vivacious books and internationally renowned bibliophile,[7] yet his article argued that books would become obsolete in the face of new technologies. In answer to the question '...how it will be with letters, with literature and books a hundred years hence?' Uzanne replied:

> If by books you are to be understood as referring to our innumerable collections of paper, printed, sewed, and bound in a cover announcing the title of the work, I own to you frankly that I do not believe (and the progress of electricity and modern mechanism forbids me to believe) that Gutenberg's invention can do otherwise than sooner or later fall into desuetude as a means of current interpretation of our mental products. Notwithstanding the enormous progress which has gradually been made in the printing-press [...] it still appears to me that the art [...] has attained its acme of perfection, and that our grand-children will no longer trust their works to this some-what antiquated process, now so very easy to replace by phonography, which is yet in its initial stage, and of which we have much to hope.

Opposite page:
Doves Press, *Paradise Lost*, T J Cobden-Sanderson and Emery Walker, London, 1909. The gold burnished lettering by Graily Hewitt was used on only three (of twenty-two) copies printed onto vellum. This heading (and the near identical headings on the other vellum copies and the 300 copies printed on paper) was designed by T J Cobden-Sanderson and written by Edward Johnston. The finished design was then cut in wood and printed in red.

Emery Walker had been typographic advisor to William Morris's Kelmscott Press before he set up this fine-press enterprise in partnership with the bookbinder Cobden-Sanderson. It was the books of the Doves Press that inspired the revival of private-press printing in the 20th century.

Uzanne's article was, more likely, intended as satire and a warning and rather less as a prediction, but the similarity of his 'miniaturized gramophone' (described elsewhere in the same article and to be made by watchmakers and using 'small cylinders as light as celluloid penholders') to the iPod, has given Uzanne's description of future 'reading receptacles' considerable advocacy. In the same year of Uzanne's cautionary tale, the *New York Times* described him as '...the best authority that book lovers know on subjects specially interesting to book lovers'.[8] Doubts over Uzanne's intentions are understandable, especially since Uzanne's article appeared at a time when the art of the printer, and the book in particular, had never been more highly regarded or its cultural influence more pronounced. Indeed, the 1890s marked the beginning of what was commonly referred to in the UK and Europe as a 'print revival' and in America as a 'print renaissance'.

PARADISE LOST
THE AUTHOR JOHN MILTON

OF MANS FIRST DISOBEDIENCE,
AND THE FRUIT
OF THAT FORBIDDEN TREE,
WHOSE MORTAL TAST
BROUGHT DEATH INTO THE
WORLD, AND ALL OUR WOE,

With loss of Eden, till one greater Man
Restore us, and regain the blissful Seat,
Sing Heav'nly Muse, that on the secret top
Of Oreb, or of Sinai, didst inspire
That Shepherd, who first taught the chosen Seed,
In the Beginning how the Heav'ns and Earth
Rose out of Chaos : Or if Sion Hill
Delight thee more, and Siloa's Brook that flow'd
Fast by the Oracle of God; I thence
Invoke thy aid to my adventrous Song,
That with no middle flight intends to soar
Above th' Aonian Mount, while it pursues
Things unattempted yet in Prose or Rhime.
And chiefly Thou O Spirit, that dost prefer
Before all Temples th' upright heart and pure,

16

Below:

Sofii Georgievne Mel'nikovoi: Fantasticheskii
Kabachek (To Sofia Georgievna Melnikova: the
Fantastic Tavern) designed and letterpress printed
by Ilia Zdanevich (more commonly known as 'Iliazd')
and published by his own publishing house, 41°
in 1919.

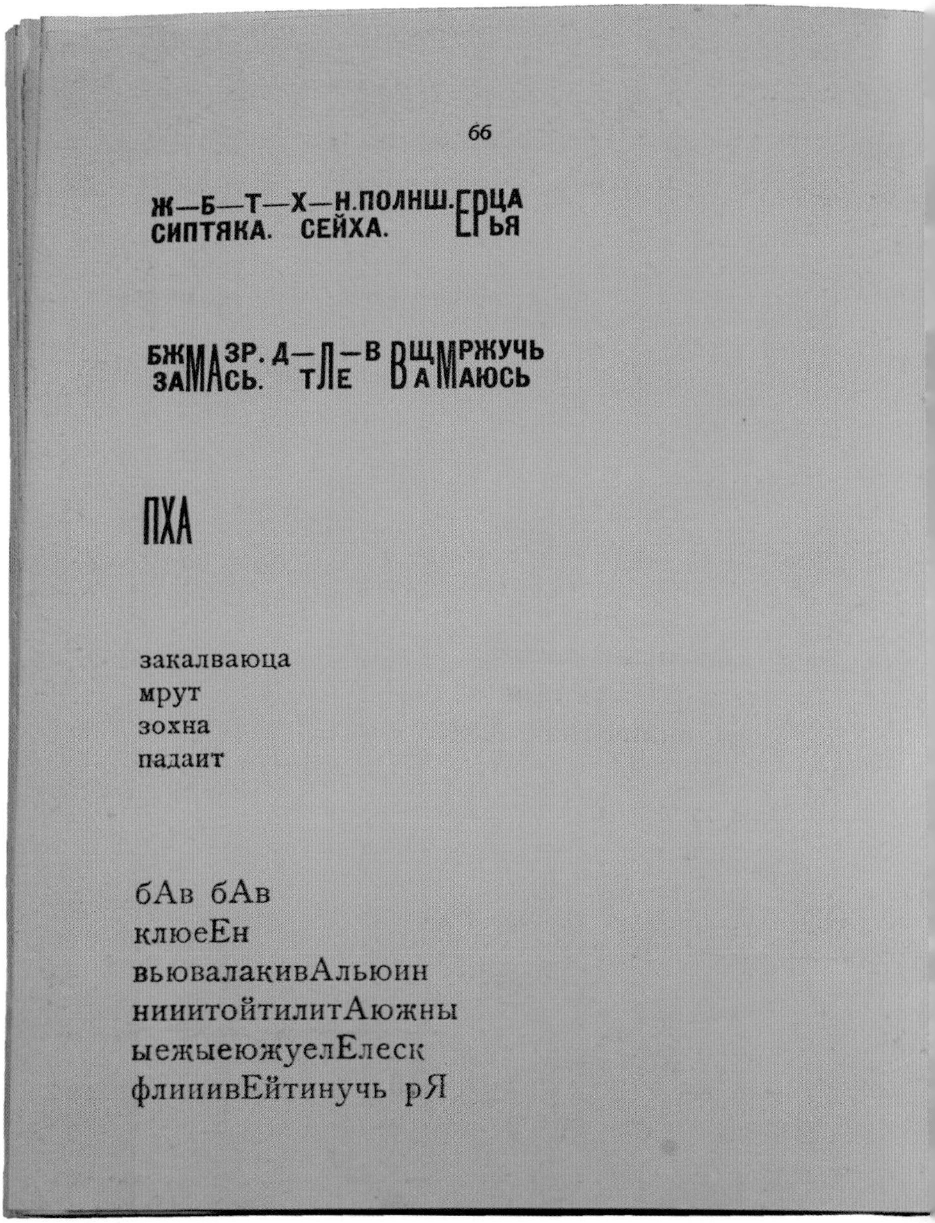

66

Ж—Б—Т—Х—Н.ПОЛНШ.ЕРЦА
СИПТЯКА. СЕЙХА. ЕРЬЯ

БЖМ ЗР. Д—Л—В ВЩМРЖУЧЬ
ЗАМАСЬ. ТЛЕ ВАМАЮСЬ

ПХА

закалваюца
мрут
зохна
падаит

бАв бАв
клюеЕн
вьювалакивАльюин
нииитойтилитАюжны
ыежыеюжуелЕлеск
флииивЕйтинучь рЯ

Print, technology and revolutions

Chapter 1: Technology as a driver of creativity
Chapter 2: Craft and technology, printer and graphic designer
Chapter 3: The business of graphic design

Below:
Kazimir Malevich, cover for Nikolai Punin, *First Cycle of Lectures Given at Short Courses for Teachers of Drawing and Modern Art*. Petrograd: 17th State Typography, 1920. Colour lithograph.

Below right:
Solomon Telingater, spread from *Kirsanov Has the 'Right of Word'*, Semyon Kirsanov (author) Moscow, 1930, printed letterpress. (Cover illustrated on the previous page.) The blue mark on the verso page is a library stamp.

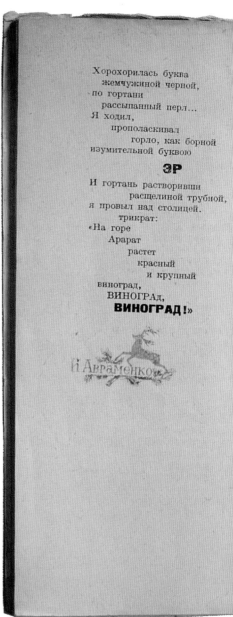

Chapter 1:

Technology as a driver of creativity

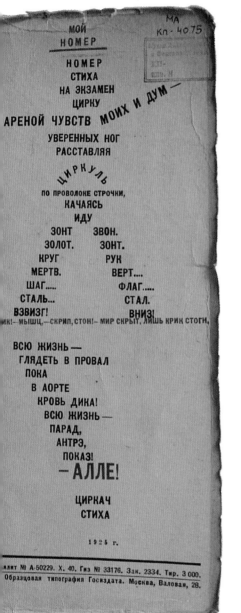

Avant Garde ideas

Because of the abundance as well as its often ephemeral nature, printed matter was recognised as being highly democratic and certainly more likely to reach the hands and minds of the general public than the contents of an art gallery. The fact that many of those artists choosing to use print media knew little about traditional typography or print would cause new ways of thinking about both the methods and the purpose of printing.

Between around 1907 and 1920, the common link between the Futurists in Italy, Spain and Russia, the Vorticists in England, the Constructivists in Russia, the Activists in Hungary, and the international Dadaists was a devotion to the 'electric wave',[9] of power driving new technologies coupled with a contempt for rational outcomes. And there can be few activities more rational than a standard page of text.

This loose collection of avant garde artists set out to defy the establishment – what it stood for and everything it valued. When they produced books or magazines the aim was that these publications should act as an antidote to those who prized the exclusivity of limited edition books bought (so the avant gardists would argue) purely for display and investment. Equally, they had little interest in practices approved by the professional printer, except when his conventions might be harnessed to further their own cause. Magazines and booklets for example, printed on cheap paper, offered art in a form that could be bought at a news stand and carried in a coat pocket to be perused on the bus or later at the kitchen table or indeed anywhere; but not in an art gallery.

Another factor that separated the avant garde from recent previous movements is that their experimental printed material was not a vehicle for 'classic' texts but, instead, carried writing that was of an equally experimental or 'transrational' nature. Texts were often political in purpose whilst their visual construct might suggest a recitation complete with expressive intonation, sound effects, etc. As a result, it was the typography itself that was a book's visual focus, rather than any separate pictorial element.

Below:
Filippo Tommaso Marinetti, front page of *Futurismo*, 1911. Print remained the favourite medium of the Futurists, and especially the newspaper because of its ability to communicate almost instantaneously to so many and so effectively.

Below right:
Filippo Tommaso Marinetti, *Zang Tumb Tumb* is a sound and concrete poem and appeared in excerpts in journals between 1912 and 1914, and then published in Milan as an artist's book in the form shown here. It is an account of the Battle of Adrianople, which Marinetti witnessed as a reporter for *L'Intransigeant*.

Futurism in Italy

The Futurists were inspired by the potential of technology – and especially electricity[10] – to change the physical world and revolutionise social order. They celebrated speed, industrial power, city life and the modern objects that encapsulated these characteristics such as the car, the aeroplane, and the modern printing press. Its founder, the Italian poet Filippo Tommaso Marinetti, used print very effectively to promote his ideas (his first Futurist Manifesto was printed on the front page of the Paris newspaper *Le Figaro*, 20 February 1909). He was also the editor of several publications, including the magazine *Poesia*, and the notorious *Lacerba* from 1914. The scale and awesome power of a commercial press, with its complex, repeated, multiple movements, speed and rhythmic noise, must surely have made a huge impression on Marinetti.

Both radio, 'talking along beams of light', and film were available and much admired by the Futurists, yet the movement's most significant legacies are in the

Below right:

A Slap in the Face of Public Taste. A book of poetry, prose and articles by David Burliuk, Nikolai Burliuk, Alexei Kruchenykh, Wassily Kandinsky, Benedikt Livshits, Vladimir Mayakovsky, Velimir Khlebnikov. Published by G L Kuzmin, Moscow 1912.

form of print. Their aim was to 'destroy the already done in order to do the very new' and yet for Marinetti the most effective method of communicating scorn and creating outrage remained print. When *Lacerba* ceased publication Marinetti moved to what would become the definitive journal promoting Futurism, *L'Italia futurista*, published between 1916 and 1918. He was also a prodigious publisher of propaganda leaflets, at one point famously climbing to the top of the clock tower in Venice to throw pamphlets (opposing the city's cultural policy) onto the crowds in the square below.

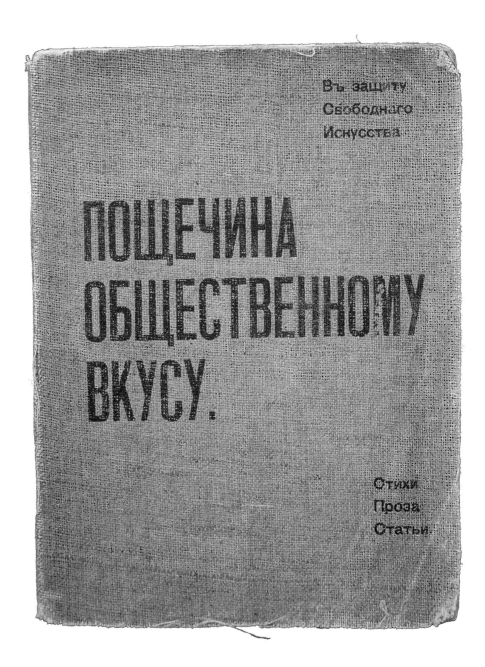

Below and below right:
El Lissitzky, *For the Voice,* Published by State Publishing House, Berlin,1923. El Lissitzky, in collaboration with the poet Vladimir Mayakovsky, used type and the full range of typographic forms and symbols to build elemental images. Each poem is introduced by a symbol on the thumb-index and occupies a double-page spread. Printed in the suprematist colours of red and black.

Russian Futurism and Constructivism

Until the October Revolution in 1917, Russian avant garde artists were sympathetic with the Italian Futurists' fascination for energy and power, but instead of glorifying specific technological trophies such as trains, planes and cars, they preferred a slower-paced engagement between man and actions – one in which human willpower remained the driving force.

In both Italy and Russia, the Futurists challenged the traditional written word by replacing linear narrative with dynamic clusters of verbal and visual signs. However, Russian Futurist books were anti-orthodox in a manner that was quite different from anything produced in Italy. In Russia, such books were distinctly pocket-sized, often made by hand with no attempt to hide the fact; the pages often being unevenly cut and roughly assembled. The handwritten, typed, rubber-stamped, carbon-copied, or letterpress printed texts and hand-coloured illustrations are knowingly crude. The cheap paper – sometimes even wallpaper or wrapping paper – individually hand-collaged covers, and stapled spines all reinforce the heightened material sense of what, precisely, was being held and the emotive relationship to the artist it provided. The human spirit and its potential was the subject. To apply the term 'book' to many of these items is inappropriate, but something one imagines their makers would happily concede.

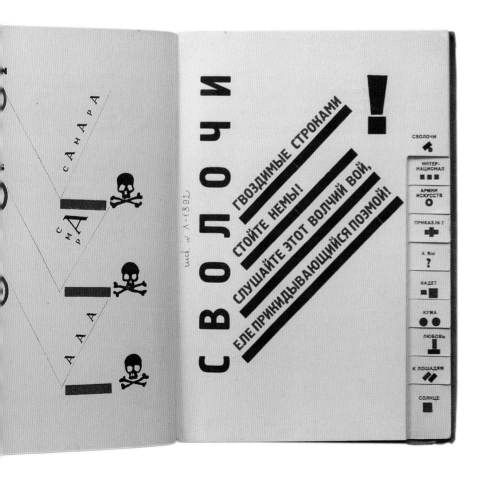

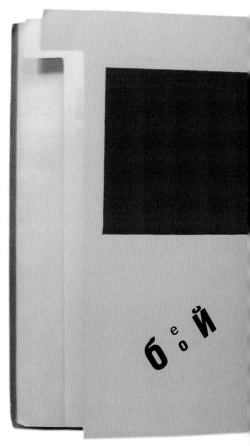

Right:
Iliazd (Ilia Zdanevich) *Ledentu le phare*. This book was published by Iliazd's own publishing house 41°, and printed at the Imprimerie Union run by émigrés Volf Chalit and Dimitri Snégaroff, who would later print all of Iliazd's French livres d'artiste. Paris, 1923.

Below right:
Cover, *Game in Hell*, (second edition) illustration by Kazimir Malevich, with text handwritten by Alexei Kruchenykh. St Petersburg, printed by Light Lithograph Printers, 1914.

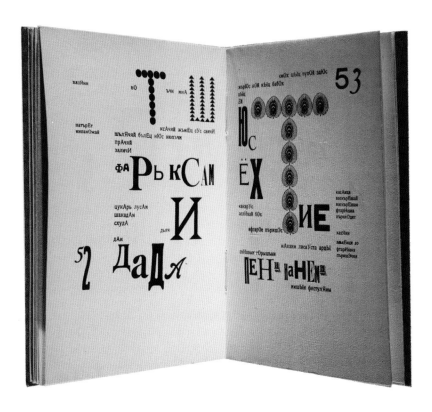

After the Russian Revolution (an event applauded by the Italian Futurists) the rough-hewn, intentionally anarchic work of poets and artists now had to be more 'responsible'. Determined by a political and social ideology dictated by official sources, Constructivist books began to show an attempt to propagate a more rational visual language appropriate to new sociopolitical preoccupations and now designed to be achieved using commercial mass-production printing technology. In 1918, a new weekly newspaper *Iskusstvo Kommuny* ('Art of the Community') was launched with a distinctive Futuristic masthead. Its aim, to bridge the gap between art and the Soviet public, was the subject of a poem by Vladimir Mayakovsky[11] titled 'Order to the Army of Art' which was printed on the first page of the first issue declaring, 'the streets are our brushes, the squares our palettes'. Art, *Iskusstvo Kommuny* stated, was 'simply work' and the artist a 'skilled technician or a constructor'[12] who 'knows his talents belong to the collective'.[13]

El Lissitzky had been an important figure of the Russian avant garde, subscribing to Suprematism, an art movement focused on elemental geometric forms. Following the revolution, he turned more to print media, and especially the design of books because '[the book] goes to the people, and does not stand like a cathedral in one place waiting for someone to approach... [the book is the] monument of the future'. recognised that the printed book was a dynamic object with a life of its own, moving from one place to another, one person to another. Its small monetary value aided this process, giving it a distinctive energy and cultural value much prized by the Constructivists.

When William Morris was planning his Kelmscott Press books he had worked in close collaboration with artists who provided the illustrative material. When Morris's contemporary, Aubrey Beardsley, artist, editor and art director was planning the next edition of his infamous journal *The Yellow Book*, the textual layout would only loosely be arranged by him, leaving its setting to be completed by the printer's compositor. In contrast, El Lissitzky sought to control every aspect of his books – both image and text. The only aspect that he could still not do himself was the actual printing.[14] The printer's workshop, for the time being, remained sacrosanct.

FREGIO ARANCIO - Dimostrazione dei Corpi

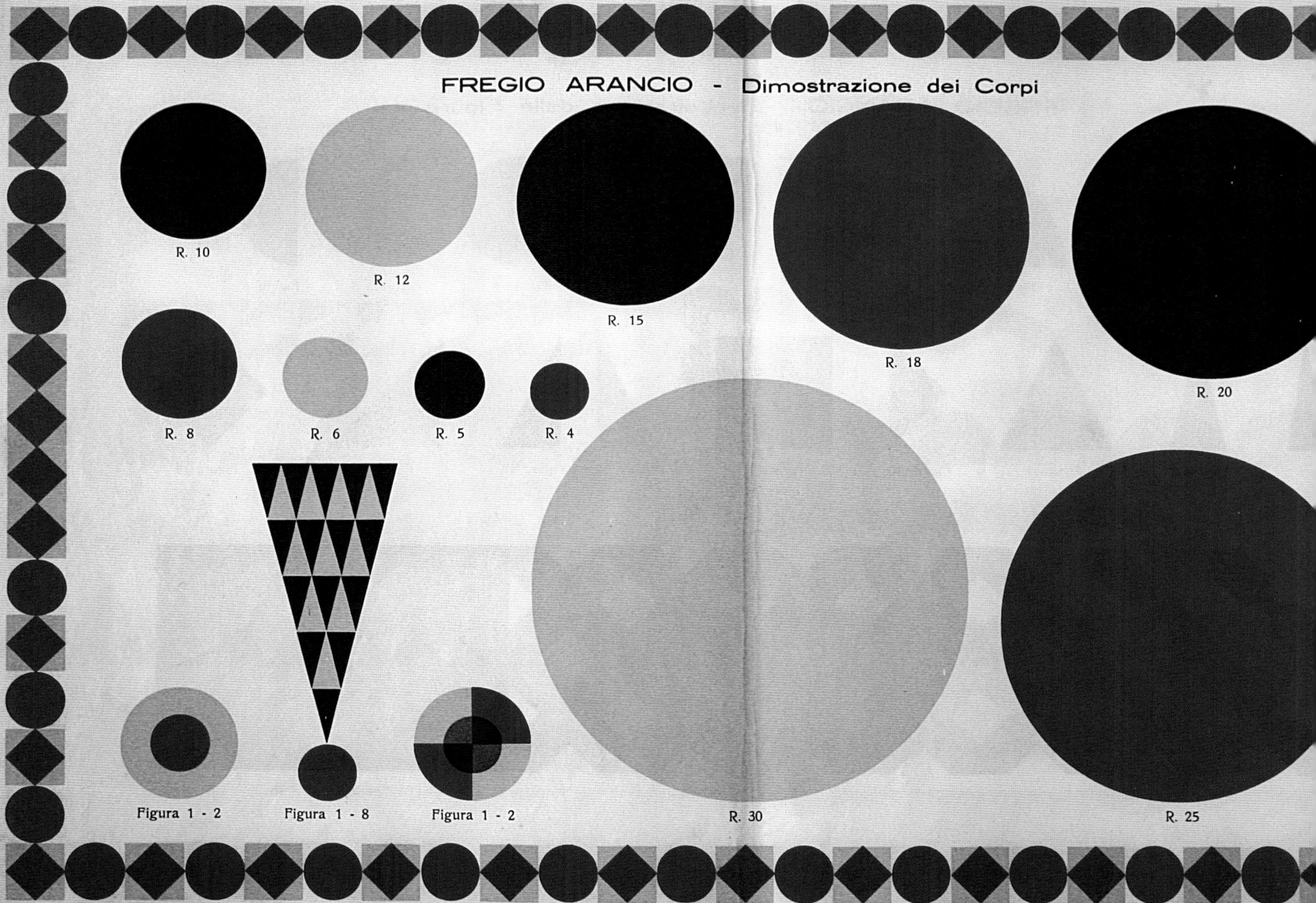

R. 20

R. 25

R. 18

R. 30

R. 15

R. 4

R. 12

R. 5

Figura 1 - 2

R. 6

Figura 1 - 8

R. 10

R. 8

Figura 1 - 2

Fregio Arancio Righe 4 - Applicazione delle Figure 1 - 11 - 15

Below:
Journal, *The Yellow Book*, designed and edited (first four volumes) by Aubrey Beardsley, 1891, the year William Morris's first Kelmscott Press book was published (see page 14). Aged just 21, Beardsley was openly critical of Morris, arguing that social and cultural issues were better served using the economies of scale – offered by commercial modes of print – and a dissolute humour.

Bottom left:
Cover of a type specimen booklet for *Satanick*, a typeface closely modelled on William Morris's *Troy* (1891) by The American Type Founders (ATF) in 1896. Legend has it that the name '*Satanick*' was the result of William Morris telling the American agent enquiring about the manufacture of an official version of *Troy* to 'Go to hell!'

Below:
Another example of the idealism of Morris and the Arts and Crafts movement being overtaken by opportunities provided by new technology. This is an advertisement designed to mimic the style of Morris's Kelmscott Press and claims that the company can manufacture the 'Embellishments and Initials shown in this specimen' at any size.

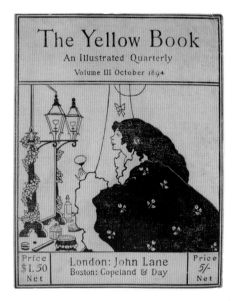

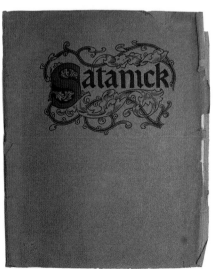

Chapter 2:
Craft and technology, printer and graphic designer

The Deutscher Werkbund

Bringing art and everyday life into closer harmony was also a key motivator behind
the Deutscher Werkbund, a group of industrialists and commercial artists/designers
whose methods and ideology were soundly rooted within a capitalist economy.

The Werkbund, set up in Weimar, 1907, aimed to promote a commercial art
based on principles that took account of modern technology, its manufactured
materials and methods of mass production. The organisation argued for a wholesale
reform of creative and economic practices and, in particular, for the linking of craftsmanship, creative endeavour, and new technology with business acumen. Further-
more, they believed the language, etiquette and ambition of the business world must
be recognised, understood and utilised by the artist if he or she was to function as
an integral part of modern society. Indeed, the 'competitive scramble' (as William
R Lethaby, Principal of the Central School of Arts and Crafts, London, disparagingly
called it) was, for the Werkbund, no longer something from which art could or
should remain aloof.

Whilst such intentions clearly distinguish the Werkbund from the ideals of the
Arts and Crafts movement, Ruskin's influence ensured that the group spent a great
deal of time struggling to adopt his moral and political concerns within their own
almost diametrically opposite stance.

In fact, in the early years of the Werkbund its leading members, such as early
commercial artists Peter Behrens and Henry van de Velde, and printer Carl Ernst
Poeschel, regularly invoked the English Arts and Crafts movement by calling for
genuine links between work and craftsmanship. Acknowledgement of Ruskin is
manifest in their call for 'joy in work',[15] a slogan which appeared regularly in early
Werkbund articles and lectures. However, this concept was answered not with
greater personal connectivity between pride, work and craftsmanship, but instead by
the collective experience of working in purpose-built factories. 'Harmonious culture'
– the rational consistency of design relating to individual companies and their
products – should, it was argued, be the required aim. A well-informed public
became the Werkbund's social and moral focus.

Nevertheless, the function of artistic endeavour remained an impassioned part
of discussions regarding a consumer-oriented capitalist economy, especially the link
between the artist and mass culture, mass communication and the newest technology.

Below:
One of many 'sample settings' for *Reclameschrift*, a 'reversed-out' condensed sans serif designed for the Klingspor type foundry (designer unknown). Despite its pared back appearance a set of decorative elements (also included in this sample) were designed to accompany it.

Bottom:
Cover, *Neu Schriften und Ornamente*, catalogue, (New Type and Ornament) Schriftgießerei Ludwig & Mayer, Frankfurt am Main, 1916.

Right:
Cover, type specimen booklet for typeface *Industria*, Schriftgießerei Emil Gursch, 1914. *(Designer unknown.)*

It was the Werkbund who, for the first time, described the activity of applied art as being something quite distinct, and very different from art itself.

The acknowledgement of 'designing', as distinct from 'applying art', was the source of a debate which came to a head during the 1914 Cologne Werkbund exhibition when Hermann Muthesius, initially a passionate arts and crafts follower (he had previously lived and worked in London and been a friend of Lethaby) now argued for the recognition of rationally assessed standards to be applied to design. He argued that the purpose of design was to facilitate the communication of manufacturer with customer, directly, honestly and efficiently. Much was made of the integrity of the designer (still regarded as an artist with specialist skills) and

Below:
Cover, type specimen book for *Reform Grotesk,* D Stempel A G, Frankfurt am Main, c. 1900. Based on the successful *Akzidenz Grotesk*, launched in 1898. *(Designer unknown.)*

Below right:
Peter Behrens, poster for an exhibition of Swiss design work to be held in Zurich.

his/her role in providing information without rhetoric – in other words, free from personal emotive ornamentation. Suddenly, 'ornament' became the focus of critical attention. Muthesius argued that since the purpose of ornament had nothing to do with function it was extraneous, and, therefore, inherently deceitful. The manufactured item, uncontaminated by human hands, was suddenly – and perversely – judged not only to be more 'honest', but also to have more integrity than its hand-made equivalent.[16]

The Werkbund now argued that modern society, must concern itself with progress by embracing technological change, not permanence. This idea of constant change; living and designing for and of the moment, left the traditional values of craft, both spiritually and practically, seemingly without a purpose. What is more, the designer's reference to tradition, craft, and to 'good practice' of the past was now considered a symptom of intellectual weakness. Instead, designers turned to machines; the dynamic embodiment of change, for inspiration.

The Bauhaus, craft and technology

On taking up his post in Weimar as Director of the Bauhaus in 1919, Walter Gropius arranged the publication of a four-page leaflet generally referred to as the *Bauhaus Manifesto and Programme*. The name 'Bauhaus' was chosen for its allusion to the masons' guilds of the medieval cathedrals,[17] a point emphasised by the placement of Lyonel Feininger's Cathedral woodcut on the cover page.

This initial approach by Gropius seems rather conservative, especially since he had been a member of the German Werkbund. His call for a 'new guild of crafts-men' to end the 'arrogant class division between artisans and artists' is closer to the ideology of William Morris and the Arts and Crafts movement than the argument for Modernism that some of his contemporaries in Germany had been calling for. 'This world of mere drawing and painting of draughtsmen and applied artists must at long last become a world that builds. In the past, when a young person who sensed within himself a love for creative endeavour began his career by learning a trade, the "artist" need no longer be frustrated because his art and skill can now be preserved in craftsmanship.' The craft workshop was to be the bridge between art and design, artist and designer, although Gropius' statement ('mere drawing and painting') leaves little doubt that design, rather than art, was the ultimate focus, and yet his appointment of artists to teach at the Bauhaus far out-numbered designers and, more remarkably, represented the avant garde of the time including Gerhard Marcks, Lyonel Feininger, Johannes Itten, Paul Klee, Oskar Schlemmer, Wassily Kandinsky and László Moholy-Nagy.

By employing such artists as part of a state-sponsored cultural programme, Gropius gave their radical ideas a 'privileged' position not accorded previously. In reply, their fearlessly innovative working methods gave the school as a whole the adventurous reputation for radical thinking that Gropius sought.

Feininger's *Cathedral,* the engraved image used by Gropius on the cover of his manifesto, was not a futuristic architectural vision but, instead, one taken from the medieval past – a Gothic cathedral – albeit within an image full of dissidence and energy. Similarly, the ideas expressed by Gropius in his manifesto were not new either. The unity of artist and craftsman had, of course, been a central tenet of the Arts and Crafts movement, and the ideals of Ruskin and Morris certainly influenced Gropius's initial plans for the Bauhaus.[18] Equally important, Gropius fully supported the Werkbund's call for the elimination of barriers between art and industry. With this in mind, teaching in the workshops was preceded by the preliminary course (*Vorkurs*). The aim of Vorkurs was to neutralise the bad habits of academic education: learning by rote, working toward preordained outcomes etc, and in so doing, liberate the creative potential of the students.

However, by 1923, the idea of a 'new guild of craftsmen'[19] had been dropped. The focus was turned to the modern world of mechanization and mass-production, radios and telephones, aeroplanes and cars, along with the use of newly efficient mass-produced man-made materials. The notion of 'masters, journeymen and apprentices' included in the 1919 manifesto was discarded and in so doing the Bauhaus helped establish a new and elevated status for the designer as a wholly

Above:
Cover for a document titled *Idea and Development of the State Bauhaus Weimar* (designer unknown) written by Walter Gropius, c.1919. The concept of 'reduction to constituent parts' is made apparent in the design of the letterforms.

Above right:
Herbert Bayer, cover for *Katalog der Muster* (Catalogue of Designs) displaying Bauhaus student work, 1925. Just six years separate these two cover designs, and demonstrates the extent to which it was Bayer's graphic interpretation of Bauhaus theory that played such an influential role in establishing the school's international reputation.

independent profession. An exhibition was mounted and a new goal was announced: *'Kunst und Technik – eine neue Einheit'* (Art and Technology – a new Unity).[20] As Gropius saw it, 'the idea of today's world is already recognisable, [but] its shape still unclear and hazy'. The role of the artist was to give modernity physical form. Like their Russian Constructivist counterparts, artists wanted to take on the roles of industrial designers, graphic designers and architects rather than 'merely' producing art for museum walls. Progress pointed toward the factory and to mass-production.

Germany's recovery from its economic problems after the First World War was due in part to financial aid from the USA but, more significantly, by importing American industrial strategies. Henry Ford's newly built, systematically organised factory in Cologne was held up as a beacon of rationality. *Rationalisierung* consequently became a fashionable concept embracing any kind of organised endeavour.

From 1923 the Bauhaus began looking for commercial commissions (this year marked the high point of Germany's inflation.) As a result, Gropius softened the School's socialist orientation (its political stance had caused the school to be referred to as the 'Cathedral of Socialism'[21]) in order to accommodate the imperatives of modern industry, capitalist enterprise, and the private patronage of celebrated American capitalists such as Henry Ford and William Randolph Hearst. 'We make our appeal to yourself [sic], who have the privilege of living in the Land whose population is today in the act of taking the reins of the Leadership of the White Race into its grasp.'

Below right:
The printing workshop at the Bauhaus c. 1923. Despite Gropius' call for a unity of art and industry the printing facilities did not take account of the mechanization of commercial printing industry. The print workshop was made up of equipment inherited from Henry van de Velde's Grand-Ducal Saxon School of Arts and Crafts, the predecessor to the Bauhaus in Weimar, and which reflected the ideology of William Morris' Kelmscott Press rather than the contemporary commercial printing office.

Opposite page:
The Bauhaus buildings, built in 1925–26, designed by Walter Gropius, and commissioned by the city of Dessau. The plans were drafted in Gropius's private office – the Bauhaus did not have its own department of architecture until 1927. Interior fittings were made in the Bauhaus workshops.

The strange ideological firmament that accompanied the Bauhaus' foray into this rather grotesque perception of the 'real' world of modern commerce demonstrates how far it had travelled since Gropius wrote in his manifesto just four years earlier: 'We perceive every form as the embodiment of an idea, every piece of work as the manifestation of our innermost selves. Only work which is the product of inner compulsion can have spiritual meaning.'

The basis for the school's current international reputation rests primarily on its achievements in Dessau. The move from Weimar to Dessau was the result of local political elections in early 1925 (the new Weimar authority was intent on cutting funding by fifty percent). However, the standing of the Bauhaus' was already sufficient for several cities to offer incentives to be its new location. That Dessau, an aspiring but mid-sized industrial city in central Germany was chosen over, for example, Frankfurt, was due to it offering Gropius the opportunity to design a new Bauhaus building. The gleaming result, opened in 1926, became an immediate icon of modernity whose expanse of glass gave the Bauhaus workshops a bright, clean and precise aspect. Le Corbusier summed up the spiritual and universal aspect of

Modernism when he said, 'No more dirty, dark corners. Everything is shown as it is. Then comes inner cleanliness'.[22]

Graphic design was not, initially, part of the Bauhaus programme and the choice of typeface for the 1919 manifesto (a quaint Art Nouveau-flavoured font popular at that time called *Ohio*) suggests a certain naïvety by Gropius regarding the communicative potential of typography. This began to change when Moholy-Nagy joined in 1923 (replacing Itten) whose interest in photography and its practical application to printed material encouraged a broader interest in the use of printed communication. Two years later, lettering classes, taught by Joost Schmidt, became an obligatory part of *Vorkurs* whilst Herbert Bayer was placed in charge of the new Printing and Advertising course. Both had previously been taught by Moholy-Nagy at the Bauhaus.

Under Schmidt, students sought the basic form of letters, in particular the circle, square and oblong. Herbert Bayer, who had impressed by his success in completing several high-profile commissions whilst still a Bauhaus student, was invited by Gropius to become a member of the teaching faculty. In the same year, and at

Gropius's request, Bayer began on work to design a typeface that the Bauhaus could use in all its communications. The result was *Universal*, a typeface built on a strict geometric grid. Bayer's methodology neatly aligned with Bauhaus strategy: make the underlying structure unambiguous and clarity of purpose will prevail. As its name suggests, the intention of *Universal* was that these 'reformed' letterforms – lowercase only, sans serif, monoline, their formulation having meticulously stripped away the myriad subtle interventions 'complicating' the typefaces cut by the craftsmen of the previous 450 years – might be validated and standardised internationally.[23] *Universal*, like other experimental 'elemental' typefaces designed at this time (for example, by Josef Albers, a fellow tutor and ex-Bauhaus student, and Van der Leck and Van Doesburg, both founder members of De Stijl), were never put into production.[24]

In his 1925 extended essay titled 'Contemporary Typography: Aims, Practice, Criticism', Moholy-Nagy predicted the replacement of typographic communication by sound recordings and film images. New ideas, he argued, needed new technologies that offered new visual experiences if they were to be communicated effectively. This could be perceived as a criticism of the Futurists for their use of 'old technology' – print – with which to express their ideas (although, of course, Moholy-Nagy was now doing precisely the same). He also predicted that 'pages of grey text' will be

transformed into colourful narratives closely connected into a dramatic whole, something similar to the experience of watching a film, but on the pages of a book. This mirrors the statement by El Lissitzky who imagined that the 'printed surface' could be transcended by 'The electro-library'.[25] Ideas such as these had been much discussed at the turn of the century and discussed by Octave Uzanne (page 14). It would be a further 70 years before technology enabled something akin to Moholy-Nagy's ideas to be made possible.

Typography as it was taught and practiced at the Bauhaus never strayed far beyond the necessary showmanship of posters, book covers and exhibition invitations. Despite Gropius' intention that the Bauhaus should actively bring about a reconciliation between 'creative artists and the industrial world', no meaningful attempt was made to loosen the cultural, practical or technological barriers that existed between designers of print and the printing industry itself. Meanwhile, the work produced by students in the 'fully equipped print workshop' (page 34) was limited to display rather than textual material, indeed, there seems to have been little or no interest at the Bauhaus in reforming the state of typography for reading purposes or, indeed, interest in current the various technologies employed in the making and manufacture of type or of printing.[26]

Elsewhere, however, colleges in which the teaching graphic design played a part were building closer practical connections to the printing industry, especially in relation to the application of current printing technology. In such cases, although determined to make design reflect the spirit of the present graphic design tutors also wanted to take the traditional craft skills and knowledge of the master printer with them.

Die vornehme Dame
und der elegante Herr
verwenden »Bajardi«
ein Hauch aus Indien:
das neue Parfüm von

abcdefghi
jklmnopqr
stuvwxyz

Below and opposite:
Cover and individual sheets of a folder probably designed by Heinrich Jost, art director of the Bauer Type Foundry in Frankfurt am Main, promoting *Futura*, a typeface designed by Paul Renner in 1927. Jost had been a pupil of Renner's at the Debschitz Schule.

A German alternative to the Bauhaus

Paul Renner in 1926, already a renowned designer and moderniser, (and working on his typeface *Futura*) was appointed Principal at the Munich Graphische Berufsschule (Printing Trade School)[27] and two months later he invited Tschichold to join his faculty to teach 'the art of typography and calligraphy'. Renner was possibly impressed by Tschichold's work on the special issue of the journal *Typographische Mitteilungen* subtitled '*Elementare Typographie*' (Elemental Typography) whilst Tschichold is reputed to have admired Renner's 1922 book *Typografie als Kunst* (Typography as Art). Both also admired the work of Edward Johnston,[28] who had led the historically based revival of formal writing as well as design the sans serif font for the London Underground, and Rudolf von Larisch whose interest was in the expressive graphic power of letters. Considering the age difference – Renner 47, Tschichold just 24 – they shared a remarkable amount of common ground.

Renner had been an early member of the Werkbund and like many fellow members was inspired by the work and working methods of William Morris. He even considered setting up a private press with Emil Preetorius, a Munich illustrator and Kurt Wolff later a publisher, although nothing came of it.[29] Renner trained as a fine artist at the Art Academy and then, in 1906, spent a year at the Debschitz

Schule, both in Munich, the latter being a pioneering school in applied art in which students learnt in workshops to design for manufacture. One of the specialised areas of study was *Grafik*, described as: 'drawing, illustration, graphic art for printing, book decoration and typography'. From here onward, books and their design would remain a principal preoccupation for Renner.

Tschichold's appointment and the specific teaching role he was offered by Renner makes clear that for both men an understanding of traditional craft and its influence on the complex structure of letterforms and their ultimate function was essential. Renner, of course, was aware that his insistence on the practical study of letterforms through calligraphy was not 'fashionable' – by this time the Bauhaus' reductive exercises in constructing letterforms from simple geometric forms was well known – but Renner believed that exploring the form and function of letters via hand-drawn calligraphy remained the most effective way of understanding letterforms, typography and the structural design of a page 'from the inside out, so to speak'.[30]

Although there was no doubt that both Renner and Tschichold were committed to designing and using typefaces that expressed ideology belonging to the present they did not consider that this meant also dismissing the past. Tschichold's classes

were intended to provide the students with a bridge from the present to the master calligraphers, punch-cutters and printers of the previous 450 years.

Renner's school, like the many other excellent German 'vocational' schools, rarely figures in conventional design histories. Yet its reputation at the time was remarkable, attracting students from all over Europe, in particular Scandinavia and Switzerland.[31] Predictably, the design work of the students displays a degree of influence of their tutors, but more importantly it demonstrated a flexible and intelligent adaptation of modernist style and method to solve commercial printing tasks. In contrast, the enduring reputation of the Bauhaus for bold and innovative graphic design is based almost exclusively on those compositions designed by its teachers such as Moholy-Nagy, Bayer and Schmidt.

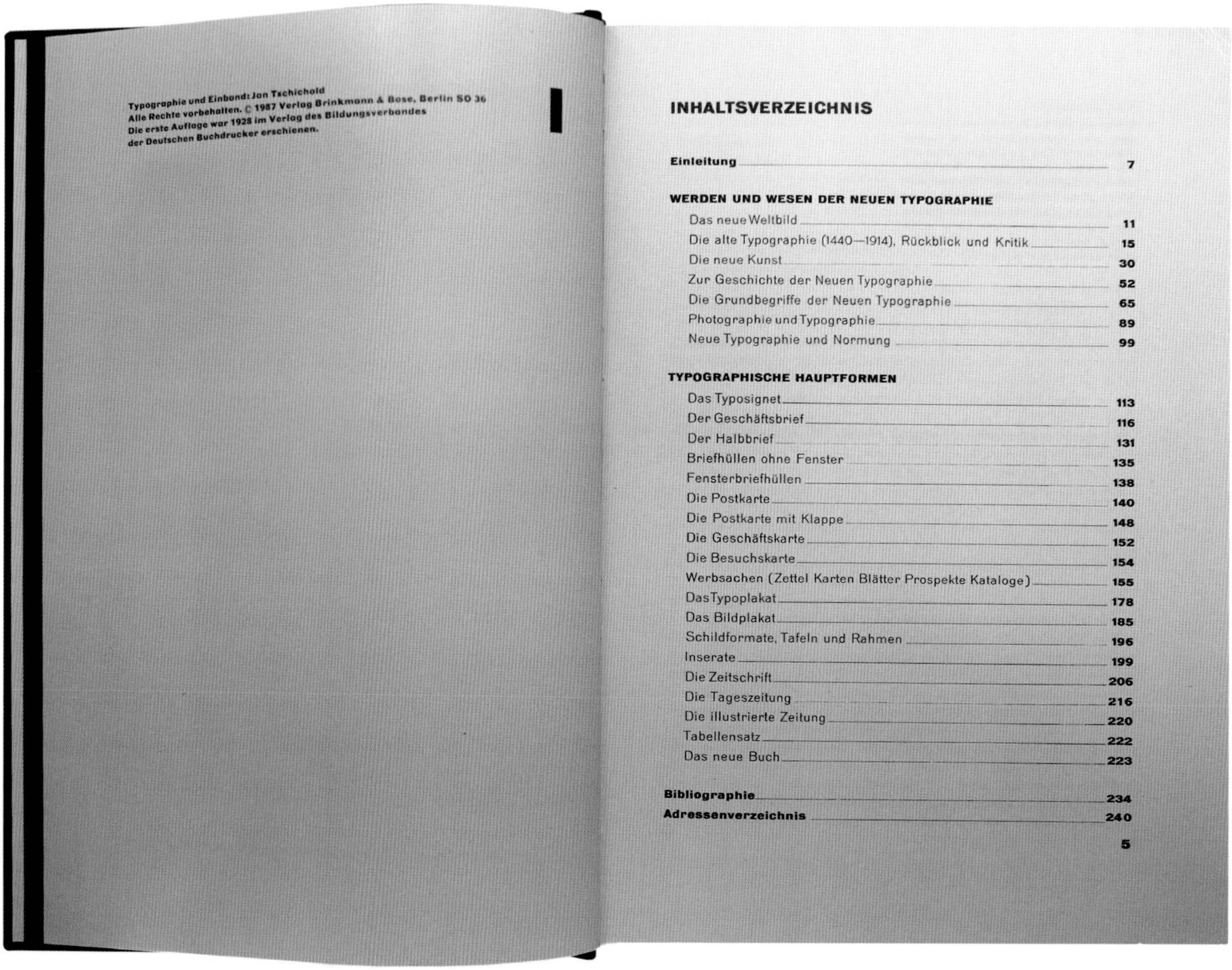

INHALTSVERZEICHNIS

New Typography

Allegiance to the printing fraternity separates Tschichold from the Bauhaus
artists and designers whose work so fascinated him. His father was a sign writer
and, as a result, Tschichold was captivated by the communicative potential of hand-
drawn letterforms from an early age. He studied at the Leipzig Academy of Graphic
Art and Book Crafts where he became immersed in traditional calligraphy and
typographic theory. Later, as a graduate student Tschichold was taught by Walter
Tiemann, a deeply respected German type and graphic designer steeped in the
history and craft tradition of German printing.

It is not surprising therefore, that until the age of 22, Tschichold's typographic
work had been conservative, though not entirely traditional. He was already
collecting the work of 15th century Italian calligraphy masters such as Ludovico
Arrighi and Giovanni Antonio Tagliente, and the 18th century types of the French
Didot and Fournier family foundries.

But, in 1923, everything changed when he visited the Bauhaus exhibition at
Weimar. It was a revelation and for the next five or six years he became a major
propagandist for the new movement in typography, travelling across Europe to
give lectures, soaking up everything he could find about avant garde artists, and
particularly the Constructivists, and applied his own work to their theories. When
offered the guest editorship of *Typographische Mitteilungen* (October 1925) he took
the opportunity to explain the origins of the avant garde and set out to persuade the
print trade of the potential role of these ideas in contemporary everyday typography
and printing. He called it '*elementare typographie*'.

Tschichold's special issue provoked considerable debate in subsequent issues and
he followed it, in 1928, with his book, *Die Neue Typographie* (The New Typography)
published by the educational wing of the German printing trade union – which also
published *Typographische Mitteilungen*. That a print union was willing to support
the author (and a *designer* no less) of such radical ideas says a great deal about the
enlightened state of a confident German printing industry. It also says much about
the success of Germany's print education system, exemplified by Renner's own
Munich Graphische Berufsschule, where design and communication theory played
such an an influential role. Tschichold's links with the print industry certainly gave
deeper credence to his argument – a depth of understanding the avant garde artists
inevitably lacked.

In *Die neue Typographie*, Tschichold argued that each age has its own unique
spirit or zeitgeist, and that design must play its part in the process of establishing
that spirit. This is in line with Gropius' call for designers to provide form for 'the
idea of today's world' (see page 32). At a time when new and ever-more efficient
methods of mass production were being devised Tschichold argued that to remain
relevant, typography must now embrace this innovative industrial culture and strive
to be evermore economic, efficient and precise. To support his argument he pointed
to the rationality of the engineer whose work, he argued, was distinguished by an
absence of historic cultural clutter enabling him to devise 'pure constructional forms
that correspond to the functions of the object'.

Opposite page:
Cover detail, *Typographische Mitteilungen* July 1928.
This was the monthly journal of the German Printer's
Association. First published in 1903 in Leipzig, it was
a rather conservative publication.

But following the October 1925 issue, when Jan
Tschichold was invited to be its guest editor/designer
and showcased work of the Bauhaus, DeStijl and
Constructivism, the journal began to reflect these
more 'progressive' tendencies.

However, Tschichold was clear that history was never irrelevant, nor were all previous typefaces inherently bad. What Tschichold argued against was the recycling of historic forms to impulsively and irrelevantly decorate contemporary printed matter. So, for Tschichold, William Morris's retreat to medieval craft values was a 'false' reaction to the degradation of the contemporary craftsman by mechanization. The 'book artists', as Tschichold describes them (usually between ironic quotation marks), who took their inspiration from the English private press movement and remained focused on the tools, presses and aesthetics of the past, were simply irrelevant. Not surprisingly, Tiemann was particularly disappointed to read these comments.

Within a few years of *Die Neue Typographie* being published politics in Germany changed dramatically. On rereading his text, and particularly in the light of increasing dominance and the levels of violence by members of the Nazi Party, Tschichold became uneasy with the restrictions he had placed upon human aspiration. It is not surprising therefore, given his understanding and appreciation of fine typographic craft, that Tschichold would recant his earlier youthful ideology – much to the incredulity of his modernist colleagues.

TYPO
GRAPHISCHE
MITTEILUNGEN

ZEITSCHRIFT DES BILDUNGS
VERBANDES DER DEUTSCHEN
BUCHDRUCKER · SITZ BERLIN

XXV. JAHRGANG
JULI MCMXXVIII

HEFT 7

Below:
Eduardo Garcia Benito, *Vogue*, 1931, an example of the decorative French New Art Deco style predominant in the USA prior to it discovering Bauhaus functionalism.

Below:
Emil Schulthess, *Du* magazine, Zurich, 1955. From a Europe still struggling to recover from the destruction of the Second World War, the positive exuberance and sheer excess of the American urban metropolis was hard to resist.

Opposite page:
Cover of the catalogue to the Bauhaus exhibition held at the Museum of Modern Art (MoMA) New York, 1938. Edited by Herbert Bayer, Walter Gropius and Ise Gropius.

Chapter 3:
The graphic design business

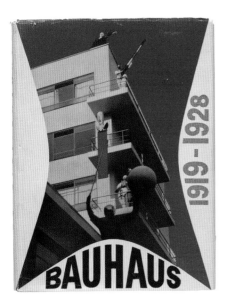

Modernism and America

'Amerika' or, more specifically, its (relatively) new and ever-changing cosmopolitan centres such as New York and Chicago, had always had a strong allure to modernisers in central Europe and when, under a strengthening Nazi regime, emigration became a necessity, America became a natural destination. Indeed, it was in New York in 1938 that the mythology and iconic status of the Bauhaus was established with an exhibition organized there by Gropius and designed by Bayer, and held at the Museum of Modern Art in New York. Probably even more influential was the book that followed.[32] In this book, *Bauhaus 1919–1928*, (as with the exhibition) Gropius and colleagues from his years as the school's Director, presented an account of the Bauhaus in which clarity of purpose was ensured by glossing over the early medieval-inspired arts and crafts period in Weimar. The success of their account can be seen in the fact that today, 'Bauhaus' and 'modern' are synonymous terms.

Modernism ('the transient, the fleeting, the contingent'[33]) first gained momentum in America after the First World War, given political traction by the desperation of economic depression and the threat of 'creeping socialism'. But the spark that ignited the modern design movement in America occurred in 1925 when the hugely ambitious Paris Exposition Internationale des Arts Décoratifs et Industriels Modernes offered the USA, who had been a major First World War ally, a prime site. This remarkable showcase would provide participants with an opportunity to demonstrate the skills, enterprise and latest technological achievements of their nation's designers, craftsmen and manufacturers. The organizers, however, stipulated a crucial condition: works submitted must demonstrate 'new inspiration and real originality' and be representative of 'the modern decorative and industrial arts. Reproductions, imitations, and counterfeits of ancient styles are strictly prohibited'. After consultation with major figures in the arts and education worlds, it was concluded that there was no modern art or design in America and so, remarkably, the United States declined the invitation.[34]

This was the alarm call American designers and, importantly, political and industrial leaders required, and over the next fifteen years dramatic changes occurred. Not only designers and manufacturers, but also department stores, museums and art galleries joined in the effort to encourage and promote innovative work and overcome the generally conservative and historically oriented consumer taste in America.

Below:
The cover of *Picture Post* magazine depicting British soldiers, October 1939. The innate and unambiguous nature of this photograph contrasts with the way the medium was being manipulated by designers and art directors in mainland Europe (see below right).

Below right:
Cover of the magazine *VU,* with the subheading 'He has won!', before the plebiscite of 12 November in Germany which led to Hitler's seizure of power. November 8, 1933.

Opposite page:
Cover, *Harper's Bazaar,* 1944 and Alexey Brodovitch (front right) and editor Carmel Snow (sitting behind the desk between two assistants) study the layout designs of the magazine spread across the floor. December 1952, New York.

A pioneering spirit was required. The arrival of Bauhaus emigrants in the 1930s was timed to perfection.

The cultural embrace of Modernism in America was firmly endorsed by the opening of the Museum of Modern Art in New York, 1929, and its exhibition *Machine Art* in 1934 was a huge and popular success. The Modernism it promoted was derived from Bauhaus functionalism, as opposed to the more elegant and more decorative French modern style that had previously dominated. American Modern was viewed as efficient, practical and convenient – a celebration of progress, the newest technology and dynamism of urban life. But significantly, American Modernism also remained effervescent in spirit, incorporating a self-referential humour and sense of play – often surreal, discordant, spontaneous, always inventive and often colourful – especially in the design of printed matter. Nowhere was this better demonstrated than in the design of the popular culture and fashion magazines. And the best of these was *Harper's Bazaar.*

Popular magazines were being revitalised by advances in technology. At the beginning of the 1930s letterpress still dominated magazine production world-wide although its command was under threat. Letterpress could, of course, print type

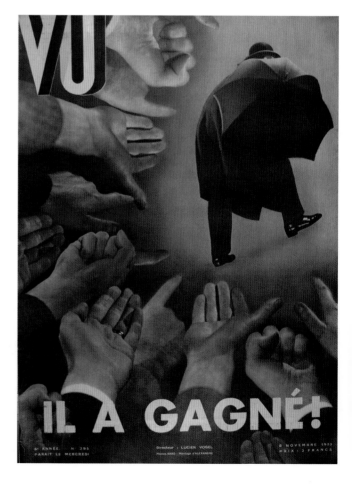

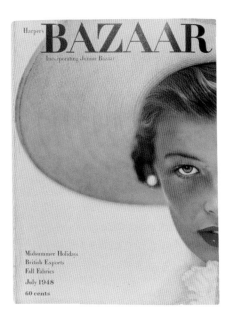

beautifully, but despite heroic efforts it could not offer full colour at a high quality. The half-tone dot was too coarse to show detail and its printing presses were never developed to print the four colours necessary for full colour work in one pass. This was important in the days before humidity control without which paper could distort between print runs making precise registration impossible. However, gravure, a relatively new printing process, was capable of printing photographic images of a consistent quality at high speeds – and large print-runs. And because gravure is capable of transferring a generous amount of ink to the paper (due to the development of quick-drying inks) it could achieve remarkable levels of colour density, intensity, tonal range and detail. The disadvantage of gravure is that *all* printed areas, including type, is printed as (very small) dots. But since the popular fashion magazine editor's priority was the photographic image, gravure became the print medium of choice.

The level of detail achieved by the gravure process encouraged designers to use photography in new and inventive ways, in particular, larger, often full-bleed images, areas of which might be out of focus, blurred images depicting moving crowds, a juddering view from a moving taxi, or by placing images immediately adjacent

Below:
Alvin Lustig, experimental letterforms using
letterpress geometric typographic ornaments, c. late
1930s. This experimental typeface led to the design
of the masthead of the influential journal *Arts &
Architecture*. Lustig's methods are unreservedly
influenced by Bauhaus methodology – and which
Lustig was happy to concede.

Bottom:
Alvin Lustig, cover design for *Industrial Design*
magazine, 1954.

so that their contents blend and boundaries become ambiguous. It was Alexey Brodovitch, Art Director of *Harper's Bazaar* from 1934, who more than anyone energized the way photography was used in magazine layout. Brodovitch had emigrated from Russia to Paris where he had had a number of jobs, including painter of backdrops for Diaghilev's Ballets Russes, poster designer and layout artist for the art journals *Cahiers d'Art,* and *Arts et Métiers Graphiques*. On his arrival in America in 1930, he made an almost immediate impact – seven years before Gropius and Moholy-Nagy.

Brodovitch would remain with *Harper's Bazaar* for twenty-five years. The magazine's influence on editorial conception, design, style, and visual intellect was felt not only in the publishing industry but across all fields of visual communication. Brodovitch brought an entirely new sense of organisation, cinematic in its sense of narrative, line, accent and form, and established the role of the Art Director as equal to that of the editor. *Harper's Bazaar* became a truly cosmopolitan publication by Brodovitch's combining of the best European and American photographers, artists and designers of the time: Salvador Dali, Man Ray, Irving Penn, Cartier Bresson, Christian Berard, Jean Cocteau, Richard Avedon, Cassandre, Feliks Topolski and Saul Steinberg.

Mature Modernism and integrity

Growth in the use of print media and the emergence of television after the war heralded a new era for advertising. It was recognised that the increasing globalisation of trade, the growing number and power of multinational corporations and an awareness of the need for large and complex organisations to be 'intelligible' in foreign or unfamiliar markets was essential to future success and growth. Controlling the way an organisation was perceived by the public via mass media fell to graphic designers in design consultancies, who effectively accepted the role of 'communications management'. This activity represented a far closer, if not a fully integrated alliance between designer and client. The fact that commercial organisations were paying large amounts of money for such a service did not go unnoticed either. In the 1920s the graphic designer could describe his role as being that of a principled, independent communicator – as perceived by the Werbund – acting in the service of the public. By the 1950s that role had shifted, graphic design was now more likely to be perceived as being in the service of the commercial sector.

Graphic design had evolved, 'come of age', and was now playing a prominent and influential role in a buoyant post-war American economy. Paul Rand more than any other American designer represents this celebrated period. His early successes were, like his heroes in publishing, achieved working for *Harper's Bazaar, Apparel Arts* and *Direction* magazines. But what elevated the status of graphic design, certainly within the business community, was Rand's hugely successful corporate identities, many of which remain in use today. IBM, ABC, UPS and Enron, among many others, owe their graphic heritage to Rand. The design of magazine and book covers might be celebrated among peers in the media coterie – and they were certainly popular with

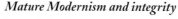

Below:
Paul Rand, IBM logo designed in 1956. Sensitively applied here (designer uncredited) on the cover of a manual for the IBM Selectric electronic typewriter in 1971.

Below right:
Bradbury Thompson, an image from *Westvaco Inspirations*, a graphic arts publication issued by the Westvaco Corporation, formerly named the West Virginia Pulp and Paper Company. Its aim was to show outstanding typography, photography, and graphic design on papers manufactured at its mills, c.1955.

an increasingly optimistic public – but the new kind of indubitable influence attained by Rand was due to his access to the nation's industrial boardrooms. One of Rand's strengths was his ability to explain to those in the business community the necessities his solution would address. According to graphic designer Louis Danziger: 'He almost single-handedly convinced business that design was an effective tool. [...] Anyone designing in the 1950s and 1960s owed much to Rand, who largely made it possible for us to work. He more than anyone else made the profession reputable. We went from being commercial artists to being graphic designers largely on his merits.' [35]

To accompany the unveiling of a new corporate identity the graphic designer also created glossy, self-congratulatory company reports. As each organisation followed the lead of their rivals, a certain predictability began to creep into corporate solutions. Simultaneously, the magazines whose covers had previously been heralded as iconic statements of 'American Modern' now began to have an achingly predictable quality. The radical aspect that had previously driven Modernism was evaporating, leaving a polished, highly refined, but essentially decorous 'mature' Modernism – precisely what the earlier European Modernists had invested so much energy in eliminating.

The over-arching control provided by communications technology: television, radio, and print, began to feed a growing concern that traditional American values, such as individual freedom and self-reliance, were under threat. The dissipating differentiation between the individual and the masses became a common theme

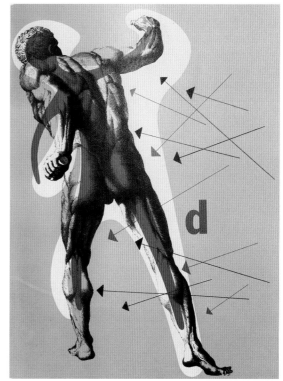

of popular fiction, typically, Sloan Wilson's *The Man in the Grey Flannel Suit*. As corporations became more powerful there was a sense that the significance of the individual was shrinking. Resistance to conformity would eventually find an outlet, ironically, utilising the very same duplicating technology that had become synonymous with large-scale corporate business.

New Wave, new technology

The close alliance of designers with corporate business, the aspiration of design company directors to feature on the cover of finance journals, the wearing of uniform pin-striped suits and bright coloured ties, had tainted the profession. The idealism that presented Modernist theory as a means of social change was, by the 1970s, long forgotten, and yet 'form following function' and its call for universal standardisation had proved a lucrative strategy. The work of international design consultancies such as Total Design in Amsterdam, Pentagram in London, and Push Pin in New York was technically sophisticated, often witty and always clever – though in a somewhat self-congratulatory manner. Their sheer size and pervading influence, together with the be-suited, groomed and corporate-aware appearance of their leading practitioners began to alienate the profession from its public service roots. There was also a new generation of young designers coming out of college who had no intention of aligning themselves with what they saw as the *business* of graphic design. The profession was in danger of eating itself. A reaction was inevitable and it arrived in the form of the underground press, psychedelia, and 'subcultural' material

Opposite page, top and middle:
Paul Rand's distinctive Westinghouse logo, an electrical manufacturing company, 1956.

Opposite page, middle:
Fifteen logos from c. mid 1960s, all very similar but for very different companies.

Opposite page, bottom left:
Total Design, a multidisciplinary design consultancy based in Amsterdam. A meeting of company principals, c. 1980, photographed by Jan Versnel.

Opposite page, bottom right:
Total Design, a spread from the catalogue of an exhibition of their work, 1983. The unusual shape of the catalogue enabled an intriguingly complex grid to be employed, although much of the work on display was for international corporate clients with predictable results.

Below:
Karl Gerstner, poster for the printing company Schwitter AG promoting their participation at a print trade exhibition, 1957.

Below right:
Ken Garland, poster, for Galt Toys, c. 1961.

predominantly in the form of posters and fanzines, all consciously designed as an antidote to the sophistication and 'ever-so-clever' wit of what was now considered to be the establishment's design fraternity.

Dissatisfaction with the status quo was made manifest in Britain in the standard manner of a manifesto. *First Things First* [36] was written in 1963 and published in 1964 by Ken Garland along with twenty other signatories. The manifesto was a reaction to the staunch attitudes held by concerned British business leaders and the 'vacuous pitches' of the visual communication industry's 'status salesmen'. It criticised the fast-paced shallow productions of mainstream advertising (and the huge amounts of money being spent) describing their intentions 'trivial and time-consuming'. The solution was to focus design on education and public service, tasks that promoted the betterment of society, preoccupations Garland suggested, more worthy of a designer's skills.

Garland, an admirer of Swiss graphic design and of Karl Gerstner in particular, spent a month in Switzerland. 'I had made Karl Gerstner's acquaintance, and he introduced me to maybe a dozen Swiss designers. I learned about their care for production values. They all knew a lot about printing and they had a personal relationship with printers and publishers. I brought that back with me.' [37]

Like Modernism, the Swiss (or International) Style was established at key schools of design – by Josef Müller-Brockmann at the Zurich School of Arts and Crafts, and Emil Ruder and Armin Hofmann at the Basel School of Design. At both centres, high standards of craftsmanship allied to a strict design rationality led to an exclusive use of sans serif typefaces, a precise (and distinctive) adherence

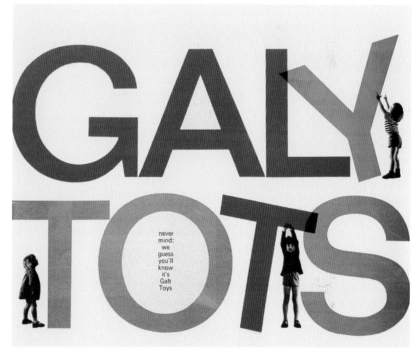

Right:

Emil Ruder, poster to promote an exhibition, *The Newspaper*, Basel,1958. The intentionally coarse half-tone photographic image in close proximity to the huge 'headline' letterform replicates the characteristics that dominate the appearance of the newspaper whilst the angle of the child's leg precisely replicates the diagonal of the Z. Printed letterpress.

Far right:

Armin Hofmann, poster to promote a ballet performance, Basel, 1959. The closeness of the hand-drawn sans serif letters for 'Giselle' echo the form of the dancer. The dot (or 'tittle') of the 'i' functions as a pivotal point for the spinning dancer and a focal point for the whole of the poster, thus uniting type and image.

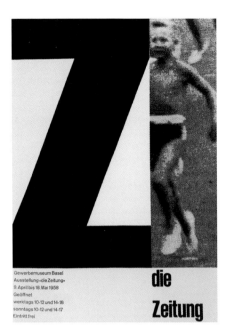

to grids and asymmetrical layouts. Textual matter, led by logic, simplicity and functionality, was set ranged left and the use of various weights of type (rather than size) used to distinguish hierarchic information: headings, subheadings, text, etc. The visual manifestation of Modernism in mainland Europe was generally austere, especially so when compared with its concurrent development in the USA.

Wolfgang Weingart, then a young German designer who had recently completed a three-year typesetter's apprenticeship in Stuttgart, went to Basel in 1964 to meet his idols, Ruder and Hofmann and, in the following year, enrolled as an independent student at the Basel School of Design. Although not a full-time student Weingart must of made a very deep impression because, in 1968, he was invited to teach typography in the institution's newly established international Advanced Program for Graphic Design.

Weingart had been experimenting with type and typography before he arrived at Basel[38] and it was his natural curiosity and questioning of the status quo that had so impressed Hofmann and Ruder. Although Ruder insisted that the primary aim of typography was communication he never excluded the potential of aesthetic effect.

On taking up his post Weingart was given complete freedom to teach the way he chose. When stripped back to essential rules and procedures typography can, he argued, be '...as boring as hell: what makes it exciting is how you interpret it [...] The moment I space out a word, I become involved in an exercise in graphics. This in turn developed into a way of teaching. I took "Swiss typography" as my starting point, but then I blew it apart.'[39] 'New Wave' was a term that had already been used to describe the radical departure of French cinema from Hollywood norms in the early 1960s. It was then used to describe the rise of Punk fashion and music in the early 1970s, and it was now also applied to the typography of Wolfgang Weingart.

Right:
Wolfgang Weingart, cover of the journal
Typografische Monatsblätter, Basel, 1973. Printed
silver and black, Weingart's design eerily predicts
the on-screen appearance of the DTP text box. The
process required letterpress set type to be printed
then cut and pasted into position before transferring
the artwork via film to lithographic plates.

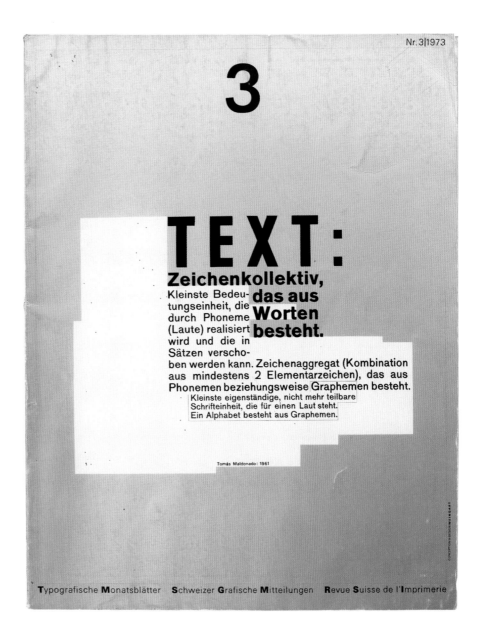

Weingart set out to explore with his students the expressive potential of
typography. Such had been the almost universal hold of rational objectivity in
European Modernism that Weingart's new work would have made an impact
regardless, but the fact that it was a typographer working in the Basel School of
Design – the very heart of the Swiss Style – it's inventive and radical appearance
was all the more astonishing.

How far could the explorative intent of the typographer progress whilst maintaining its primary typographic function? Weingart wanted to explore the semantic
function of typography: modifying the appearance of type itself and adjusting
letterspacing and wordspacing as well as the sizes and weights of individual
characters to intensify, qualify or even disguise meaning. 'What's the use of being

Below:
The first 'ATypl Working Seminar' (*Association Typographique Internationale*) was hosted by the Basel School of Design in November 1974. Weingart asked a student, Philip Burton, to design the promotional material in the typeshop. In the following year, André Gürtler, lettering teacher and committee president, invited Burton to design a 'documentary' about the ATypl seminar for publication in *Typografische Monatsblätter*.

Below right: The work of Heinrich Fleischhaker, typography tutor at Basel School of Design, *Typografische Monatsblätter*, 1981.

legible when nothing inspires you to take notice of it?' Weingart's work was always the result of a long and intensive period of rumination, as he explained,

> Creative design work wears you down physically. For a poster I need twelve weeks from the initial concept to work out all the technical details and get the film ready for press. [...] The craziest ideas come especially at night. I set them down in brief sketches and carry them around with me until I've forgotten what they were for, or I feel the time is right to make one more attempt to complete the project. This constant collecting of ideas, which are then set down in words and drawings, is an essential step towards further development. It's a way of slowly working one's way into the technical processes of the project and preparing oneself for a new encounter with technology.[40]

The appearance of Weingart's work was being compared to the results derived from early computers – computer technology was a subject much discussed and often reproduced in graphic design journals, including *Typografische Monatsblätter* during the 1970s. But as Weingart explained, his work was the result of time-consuming and painstaking work – cutting, positioning, adjusting, and readjusting the various

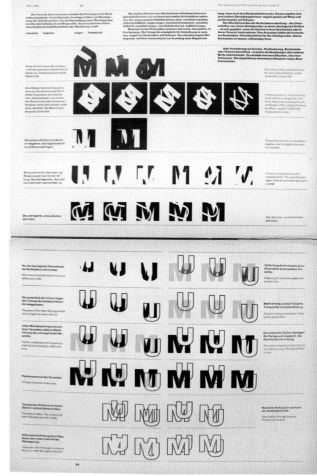

Below:
April Greiman, *Design Quarterly*, USA, 1986.
Subtitled, *Does It Make Sense?* Greiman redesigned
the magazine as a single-sheet fold-out poster.

Below right:
Dan Friedman, cover of *Typografische Monatsblätter*,
February, 1971.

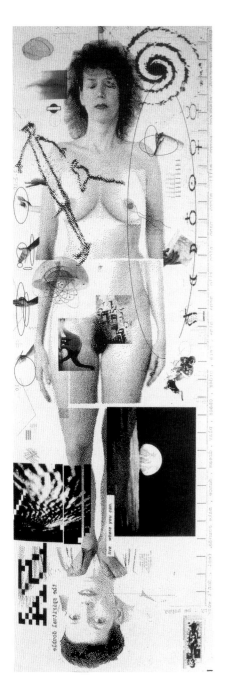

elements before being finally pasted into position. Weingart was proud of his
craftsmanship and ensured his students obtained the same essential grounding.

American students travelled to Basel to study in the Advanced Program for
Graphic Design and returned enthused by Weingart's ideas and methods. Dan
Friedman was a student there in 1968–1970, the first years of the programme. On
his return to America, Friedman taught at Yale University and then worked for
several high-profile design consultancies including Pentagram's New York office
(from 1979 to 1982). However, whilst working as an associate of Pentagram in New
York a sense of disillusionment took hold, 'In the 1960s I saw graphic design as a
noble endeavour, integral to larger planning, architectural and social issues. What
I realised in the 1970s, when I was doing a major corporate identity projects, was
that design had become a preoccupation with what things look like rather than
with what they mean. [...] We have deceived ourselves into thinking that the
modernisation service we supply has the same integrity as service to the public good.
Modernism forfeited its claim to a moral authority when designers sold it away as
corporate style.'[41]

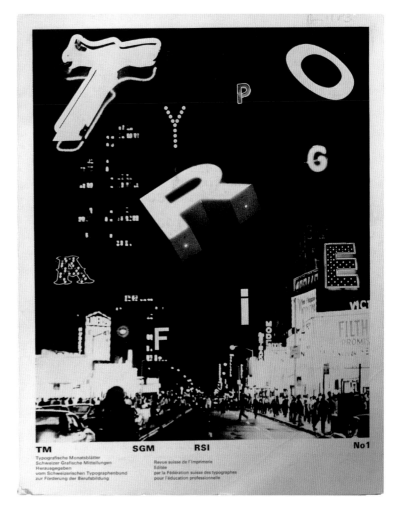

The agenda of corporate projects was highly predictable – solving the same problems with the same solutions *ad infinitum*. Friedman's concerns precisely echoed those expressed by Ken Garland in his *First Things First* manifesto a decade earlier.

New Wave represented a radical spirit that associated the idealism of modernity with a creative process reflecting that of 'fun-loving visionaries' rather than the rationality of the scientist. Another young American designer who had studied in the Basel School of Design, April Greiman, encompassed New Wave philosophy with aplomb. Having moved to California, Greiman was also an early enthusiast of the Apple Mac computer, and demonstrated its creative potential when commissioned to design an issue of *Design Quarterly* in 1986. Subtitled *Does It Make Sense?* Greiman redesigned the magazine as a poster that folded out to almost six feet in height. It included a life-size, computer-generated image of her body accompanied with images representing the evolution of communication technology. The result was shocking on several levels but most important was its unconditional celebration of a new technology which, until that point, had been a source of disquiet and even fear among many in the design fraternity. She proved that digital technology could be used intuitively, whilst the control Greiman demonstrated proved that crafts-manship could still be an integral part of the graphic designer's actions. Of equal significance, it also playfully countered the dominance of the essentially masculine stance of modernist ideology.

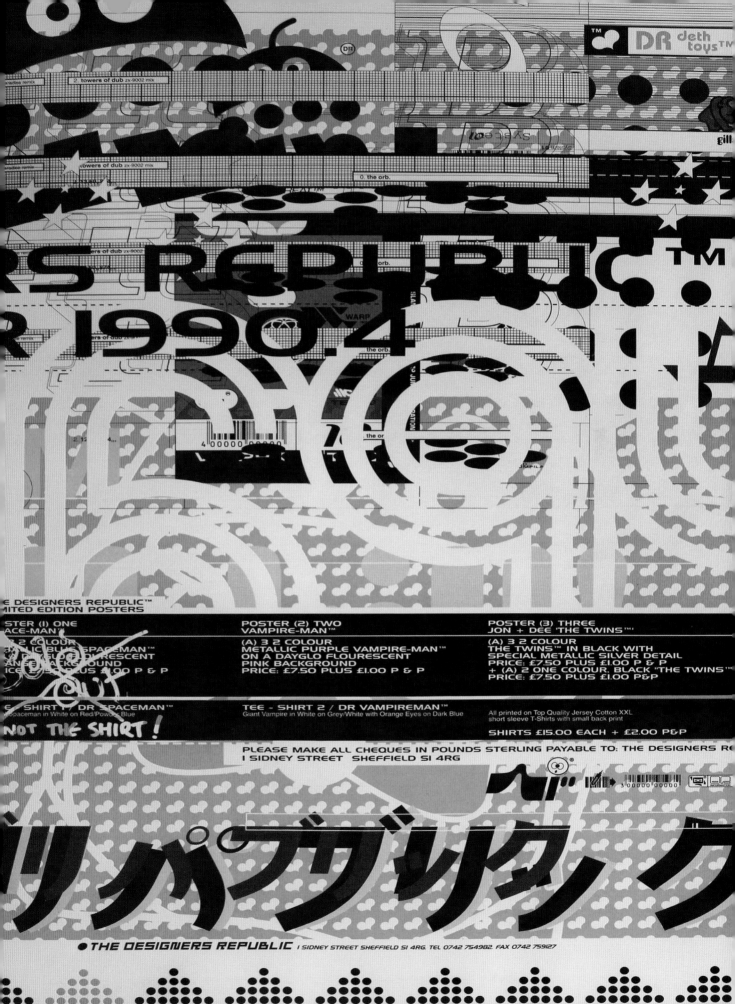

Below:
Bill Bissett, a page from *The Lost Angel Mining Company*, a hand-stapled book, typewritten and printed using a mimeograph machine at his Blew Ointment Press, Vancouver, 1969. Bissett, a Canadian poet, set up the Blew Ointment Press (also spelt 'blewointment') in 1962. Clip art, decorative material gleaned from type catalogues and found photographic material are also incorporated elsewhere in the book.

Immaterial technology in the physical world

jellokingmeetsthmandans,orwhereeveryugothereisalwaysamassacre

```
                        g
                       day
                      day day
                     day day day
                    day day day day
                   day day day day day
                  day day day day day day
                 day day day day day day day
        day day day day day day day day day
        give me land nd love
        give            yayayayayayayayayayayayayayayay
        give me
        give me land
        give me land and love
        and love give me journeys
        , journeys to secret streams give
        me love on this summer night/day day day
        day day day day day day day day day day
        this here night yay yay yay yay yay yay
        yay aya yay yay yay ya yay yay yay
          yay yay yay yay yay yay yay yay
           yay yay yay yay yay yay y
            yay yay yay yay yay yay
             yay yay yay yay yay
              yay yay yay yay
               yay yay yay y
                yay yay yay
                 yay yay yay
                  yay yay y
                   yay y
          smilin        yay   , pumpin thet organ
```

```
                             free
                             sand
                                in
                            r love
                              heat in
                                  in
                                 r
                               wagon
                                 don
                            wheel in gift
```

```
  g
 ot
ray
 s
cum
 i
 n
    me give meme
no memory

    yu
    ma
give
    me
ove give
me
nd land
ngbfaith
    stuff
  enuff
nothing
     tuff
  enuff
     gin
grrrrrrrrrrrrrrrrrrrrras
  rays
    give
 me
   me giveme
   yu lovethis   foldin
```

```
ta her
   own mother how she opins
thet organ  yay of love
                 give me this night
        this love give me and it fly away sure
yu r it yu r it flyin away give me
heart to give me to hold my faith give me th heart
to hold my faith give me th heart
to hold my faith give me th heart
to keep my face give me sum love
on this summer night and it fly
treeaway give me sum love and it
fly away give me sum there it
already flyin day day day day day day day
night night night night night night night night
yay yay yay yay yay yay yay yay yay yay yay
give me land and love
give me journeys to secret streams
give me love on this summer night
give me love and it fly away
```

Below:

An advert for the office mimeograph duplicating machine, manufactured by A B Dick. During the 1960s, direct access to mimeograph machines, letterpress and, occasionally, cheap offset lithographic presses placed the means of print production in the hands of the writer, poet, graphic designer and independent publisher. Quite suddenly, everyone seemed to have access to 'print'.

Below:

Bill Margolis, Eileen Kaufman and Bob Kaufman printing the first issue of *Beatitude,* the self-styled 'quintessential "Beat" publication', using a mimeograph machine, San Francisco, 1959. Photograph by Fortunato Clementi (from *Beatitude* number 17).

Chapter 4:
Networking before the Internet

Low tech, low cost print opportunities

The technical sophistication of commercial printing processes, to say nothing of the cost, had been a major barrier to anyone wishing to publish. But during the 1930s, 'stencil duplicating', a technology first introduced during the 1880s, was growing in popularity. Manufactured by A B Dick, the mimeograph machine offered a cheap, simple (if crude) method of duplicating material.[42]

The mimeograph worked by forcing ink through a stencil onto paper. The stencil was most commonly made (or 'cut') by the crisp metal typewriter key striking the stencil directly. The impact of the key displaced the coating, making the tissue paper permeable to the oil-based ink. It was also possible to write or draw using any sharp metal 'stylus'. During the Second World War, mimeograph machines, being lightweight, compact and relatively quiet to use, proved to be the perfect clandestine printing machine.

After the war these qualities also encouraged their use – together with all other available means – for the printing of texts forbidden by the state in post-Stalin USSR. These might be made using carbon paper, either by hand or on a typewriter as well as in conjunction with mimeograph machines. Because the raw materials required were so cheap anyone with access to an office could surreptitiously print a small 'edition'. Larger documents were printed on commercial presses during a night shift. Boris Pasternak's novel *Doctor Zhivago*, 1957, and Aleksandr Solzhenitsyn's *One Day in the Life of Ivan Denisovich*, 1958, were early examples. Before glasnost, these self-publishing and self-distributing ('samizdat') practices were dangerous because all copy machines, printing presses, and even office typewriters were officially owned and controlled by the KGB.

Over time, the crude physical state of these underground documents came to be admired for its own sake, their distinctly hurried appearance becoming a potent symbol of resourcefulness and a rebellious spirit, sharply contrasting with the appearance of commercially printed texts passed by the censor's office for publication by the state.

In the West during the 1950s, mimeograph machines were manufactured in large quantities and heavily marketed as duplicating technology for office work, classroom materials and for the printing of local newsletters and church bulletins. These machines proved so successful that manufacturers such as A B Dick in the USA

Below:

L'Incroyable Cinema, 'The Film Magazine Of Fantasy Imagination', was edited by Harry Nadler, ran for five issues from 1969 to 1971, and was printed on a Multilith 1250 press in Salford, UK. Cover illustration by Eddie Jones. Nadler, with others, went on to set up the acclaimed Festival of Fantastic Films, an annual non-profit celebration of cinema fantastique that still runs today.

Below right:

The Kim Wilde Fan Club News, 1981–1997. Explicitly DIY, such home-made magazines might be construed as an alternative to glossy pop magazines but they do not come from a counterculture position. Published by Big M Production Ltd.

began to develop simple, compact single-colour lithographic machines, epitomized by the Multilith 1250, capable of being operated with minimal training by larger organisations for in-house communications. This and similar machines encouraged the appearence of 'instant print' shops on the high street.

At the same time, a number of small amateur magazines, called 'fanzines', began to circulate, and in the early 1960s their numbers increased substantially. The fact that these were very clearly non-official, non-professional productions was no deterrent, indeed, it was the simple purpose and sheer pleasure of making them that appears to have been the key ingredient for their 'alternative' identity. But fanzines (in contrast to samizdat literature) had little or no sociopolitical intent and, generally, little or no creative ambition other than to celebrate, for example, science-fiction, horror films, popular music icons etc. Fanzines were not commercial enterprises, and most were free to anyone who provided a 'letter of comment' about the fanzine's content to the editor. Networking seems to have been a key motivation. In fact, some fanzines consisted exclusively of letters received by the editor in which discussions were conducted in much the same way as they are today in blogs, Internet newsgroups and mailing lists, albeit at a slower pace.

Below:

d. a. Levi and Kent Taylor, pages from *fortuItOns motHeRFuCer*. A mix of random newspaper sheets, typewriter, mimeograph and letterpress. Published by Levi's Renegade Press, Cleveland, 1965.

Below right:

Ted Berrigan, *The Sonnets* 1964. Cover design by Joe Brainard. This is Berrigan's self-published edition of *The Sonnets*, which would later be recognised as playing a quintessential part of Modern American literature and republished in numerous anthologies.

Rise of the Western alternative press

In the 1960s, new countercultural and revolutionary movements began to emerge that would give rise to a further transformation of alternative print, spawning countless new magazines by the end of the decade. It was initiated largely in the USA (and more specifically, New York and San Francisco) by authors and poets who, of necessity, were creating their own communities and audiences by the use of mimeograph machines, or in some cases, with direct access to letterpress or inexpensive offset lithography. (The printing industry's 'closed shop' mentality, so prevalent in the UK and Europe, was always more selectively applied in the USA.) In a very real sense, it seemed that anyone could become a publisher and hundreds did. Once the materials and tools were in their hands some found it sufficiently alluring to begin experimenting, mixing fonts, weights and sizes of type to provide additional expression for their words.

The existence of numerous independent bookstores meant that it was possible to find these publications on display, despite their raw appearance, alongside glossy commercial counterparts. But, again, it appears to be the ability to network and

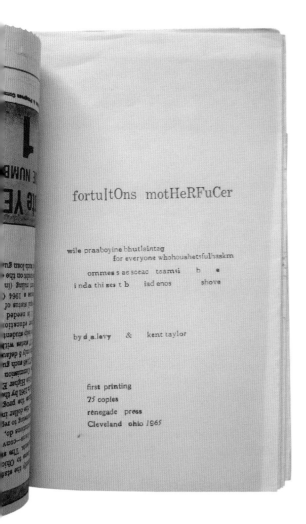

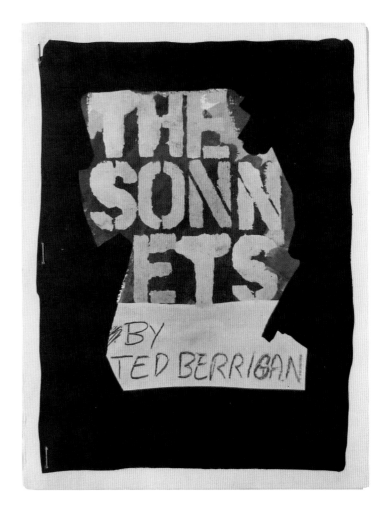

Below:

The East Village Other (*EVO*) launched in 1965 by Walter Bowart, New York, as an alternative to the newspaper, *Village Voice.*

Below right:

IT (*International Times*) was founded in London in 1966, editors and designers were numerous. Its offices were raided by the police on several occasions and ceased publication in 1973 when it was convicted for running gay contact ads.

make contact with similarly intentioned individuals, that was a key motivation: 'More important than the quality of their contents was the fact of these magazines' abundance and speed [of production]. Having them we could see what we were doing, as it came hot off the griddle. We could get an instant response to what we'd written last week, and we could respond instantly to what the guy across town had written last week.'[43]

Similar activities arose in many of the larger metropolitan centres around the world which, in turn, encouraged some to launch more ambitious publications that would become national or even international in their distribution. *IT* (*International*

Times) and *OZ*[44] were leading underground or 'alternative' publications in the UK which, despite their successes, admirably maintained their anti-establishment credentials, not only editorially – Allen Ginsberg, William Burroughs and Germaine Greer were contributors to both – but also in their increasingly adventurous design (especially Martin Sharp's work for *OZ*).

In the USA, underground newspapers were more numerous, with almost every city and college town having at least one alternative newspaper of its own. One of the most graphically innovative was the *The San Francisco Oracle*, (1966–1968) designed by Allen Cohen, in which texts were allowed to run over into photographs and illustrations causing words to sometimes all but disappear. Their printer, Howard Quinn, eventually allowed Cohen and his colleagues into his press room on Sundays to run the lithographic presses themselves. Unshackled by the need to pre-plan or explain what they wanted the printer to do, they began, for example, experimenting with the lithographic printing press by placing makeshift wooden dams in the ink fountain and using them to feed different coloured inks simultaneously through the press. The result was a multiple rainbow effect that would vary slightly as the edition progressed. Having watched the press physically transferring ink onto paper inspired Cohen to make numerous experimental trials; a creative process that gave *The San Francisco Oracle* a unique and often sensational appearance. The first issue had a circulation of 3,000, at its peak, the publication's print run was around 125,000.

An important development at this time was the Underground Press Syndicate, a network of counterculture newspapers and magazines founded in San Francisco, 1966, by five underground publishers. The idea was that any publication could join

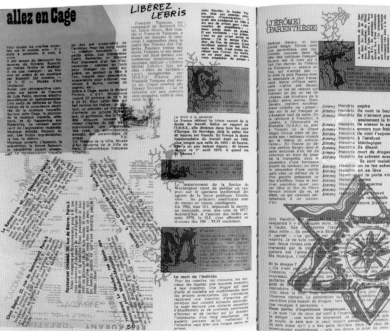

the network and that any member of the network was allowed to freely reprint the contents of any other member, making quality articles by renowned authors available to even the most modest start-up paper anywhere in the world. In the following years the number of publishers within syndicate reached over 270, in the main from around the USA, Canada and Europe. A world-wide network had been created but it was short-lived, folding shortly after 1973.

Photocopying and zines

First marketed in the 1960s by Xerox, photocopiers became available for use in offices and then to the public during the 1970s in the form of coin-operated machines in, for example, libraries and, later, in copyshops. A black and white copy of a text and/or original artwork could now be created cheaply and instantaneously. It was far cleaner and simpler to use than the mimeograph and offered infinately more creative possibilities.

As mentioned earlier, the 1970s was also the decade of Punk and the raw immediacy offered by the photocopy machine seemed entirely complimentary.

Opposite page, left:
Mark Perry, *Sniffin' Glue*, a monthly zine begun in July 1976 and released for about a year. During its early days the Punk movement was ignored by the mainstream press, whilst *Sniffin' Glue*'s circulation reached 15,000. Fearing absorption into the mainstream music press, Perry ceased publication in 1977 and encouraged others to create their own punk zines.

Opposite page, right:
John Holmstrom, design and illustration for the cover of *Punk* magazine, New York, 1976. There were fifteen issues between 1976 and 1979, followed by several occasional 'special' issues.

Right:
Jamie Reid, record cover, *Never Mind The Bollocks,* 1977. Reid had bought a printing press with which he used to produce a 'shit-stirring' community paper reporting news of local corruption. He was influenced by the Situationist art movement, graffiti and the clashing randomness of street graphics, the same anti-aesthetic so common in handmade fanzines.

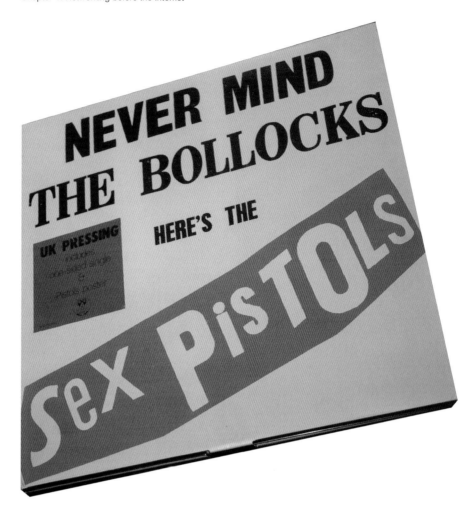

A new generation of home-made magazines, or 'zines', were defined by the felt-tip pen, Letraset (page 100) the typewriter and often included photographs and/or words cut or torn from newspapers. All of this was collated, pasted down, photocopied and stapled by the same person who would then sell them. Unlike fanzines, zines proffered equal emphasis on visual and textual material. All boundaries concerning who could or could not be a journalist, editor, graphic designer, printer, or even basic notions of what a 'publication' should look like, evaporated.

Sniffin' Glue, photocopied black and white sheets held together with a single staple in the top corner, was the first UK monthly Punk zine, started by Mark Perry in 1976 – it lasted for thirteen months. He would respond to a gig almost immediately and report it from an insider's viewpoint. The photocopier was an essential part of this process because it allowed Perry to use the most basic tools to create fast and furiously using whatever he had to hand: '[making issue number one] I had a children's typewriter plus a felt-tip pen, so that's why the first issue is how it is. I just thought it would be a one-off. I knew when I took it to the shop there was a good chance they'd laugh at me, but instead they said, How many have you got? I think my girlfriend had done twenty on the photocopier at her work and they bought the lot off me.'[45]

Below:
Stewart Brand, *The Last Whole Earth Catalog*, back cover and double page spread, 1969. Containing 448 pages, this was less a catalogue more a map for an American rite of passage, encapsulated by the saga, *Divine Right's Trip*, written by Gurney Norman, a novel that meanders through Brand's eclectic selection of 'tools' for life. Events in Norman's text are narrated by a 1963 VW camper van as it is driven across America in a haze of drug-addled scenarios before its occupants find nirvana in the form of 'The Flash' on the final page.

Opposite page, top:
Mick Mercer, inside cover page from *Panache*, (1976–1992) a twelve-page, photocopied, stapled publication, 1980.

By the 1980s, the number of publishers of zines had multiplied to the extent that a journal, *Factsheet Five*, was published in 1982 to review and catalogue their existence. Created by Mike Gunderloy in Alambra, California, it provided a networking point for zine creators and readers – often the same people. Zines of every genre were included, from perzines (a single author's own personal opinions and observations) to those that might cover an assortment of different and obscure topics. By the end of the 1980s *Factsheet Five* had established an online presence and the Factsheet Five Collection of over 10,000 zines was donated to the New York State Library in Albany, New York. *Factsheet Five* folded in 1998.

The Whole Earth Catalog

One other rather unique printed publication deserves mention because of its conceptualsimilarity to the World Wide Web. *The Whole Earth Catalog* was a soft-covered, large-format book, which appeared in several editions between 1968 and 1971. It was collated and designed by Stewart Brand and friends. The title came from

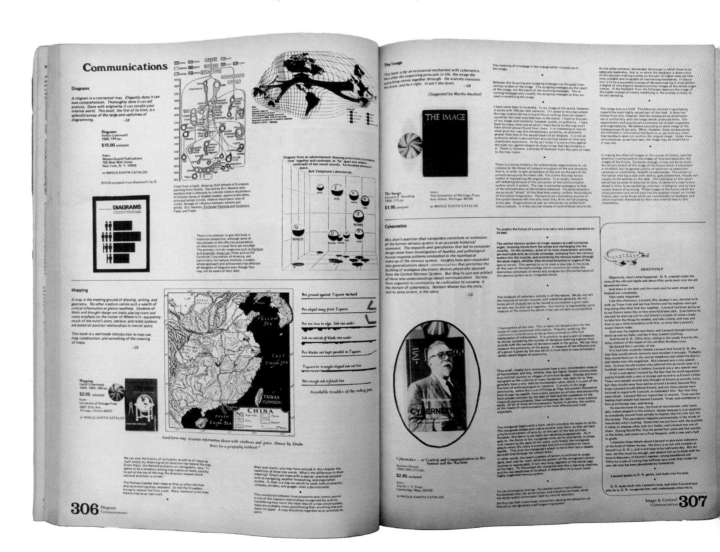

Bottom:

Michael Nicholson, cover and spread from *Bio Auto Graphic,* 2006. Nicholson's on-going series of autobiographic A5 booklets are handwritten, hand-drawn, and printed in open editions using a desktop printer. Nicholson is also a professional illustrator, designer and lecturer.

a previous project when, in 1966, Brand initiated a public campaign to have NASA release the satellite photograph of the whole Earth as seen from space. He thought the image might be a powerful symbol, evoking a sense of shared destiny and encourage adaptive strategies from people.

Several years earlier, Brand had embarked on 'a commune road trip' with a truck that was not only a mobile tool-hire store, but also an alternative lending library and, to Brand's mind, a 'micro-education service'. Brand, then aged twenty-three, called it the 'Whole Earth Truck Store'. However, his bestselling 'tool' was the printed catalogue; an extensive annotated list of tools that he could not fit in his truck. Brand decided to extend this by creating a comprehensive worldwide catalogue to provide a network not just for the world's tools, but also for ideas, skills, new technologies, inventions—including the creative output of early synthesisers and computers—that enabled everyone to 'find his own inspiration, shape his own environment, and share his adventure with whoever is interested'.

The editorial selection was eclectic, the annotation informative and opinionated, and included thousands of images. The editorial focus was on self-sufficiency, ecology, alternative education and a 'do it for yourself counterculture'. Its design was a similarly intuitive patchwork that only hinted at the possibility of an under-lying grid structure. As its title suggests, *The Whole Earth Catalog* was truly global in outlook and its growing content was revised according to readers' experiences and suggestions. Several decades later, Steve Jobs compared *The Whole Earth Catalog* to the Internet search engine Google, 'When I was young, there was an amazing publication called *The Whole Earth Catalog,* which was one of the bibles of my generation.... sort of like Google in paperback form, 35 years before. It was idealistic and overflowing with neat tools and great notions.'[46]

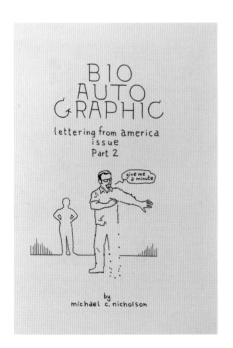

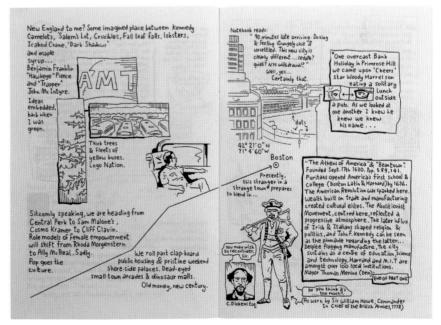

Digital technology and the zine

When computers became small and 'personal' enough to sit on desk tops, Desk Top Publishing (DTP) software became available together with black-and-white printers capable of printing A4 sheets. From here on, anyone with these 'tools' had the means to create and publish their own printed material without even leaving the house.

Initial technical limitations meant that there was a tendency for digitally made paper zines to appear familiar, even 'normal'. DTP software was designed to enable the user to produce professional (meaning conventional) looking books and magazines – qualities representing everything most zine-makers loathed. The energy that had given the strongest possible sense that nothing mattered as much as getting the words down fast and furiously had been waylaid by the DTP menu.

The economic crisis of the mid 1990s and the dramatic increases in postal charges also took its toll on paper zines. More importantly, digital technology was about to take another direction. Speculation had been rife about the 'World Wide Web' and, during the first decade of the 21st century, many zine-makers began exploring the opportunities of a web-based platform. But the pervasive sheen of the screen proved too pristine and to the surprise of many, this only reinforced the value of paper and ink. This time it was professional writers, artists, illustrators, designers, photographers as well as social and political commentators who were using their computers and desktop printers to create a new and far broader wave of independent publishers. Paper-and-ink zine culture had been reborn thanks to digital technology.

This 21st century boom in self-publishing was fuelled by a passion for the tangible, material qualities of print. 'You can't hold a blog together with tape and staples; you can't hold your zine together with CSS and HTML.'[47] However, the immediacy provided by the Internet meant that the output of these new paper-and-ink publishers need no longer be about the here and the now. Their production could be mulled over, petted and cared for, activities the pre-Internet zine publisher rejected in favour of expediency. Whilst many of these new print enthusiasts had embraced the 'zine' concept, others came to print via very different routes and, one way or another, many have since been enveloped within that broadest of labels: 'artists' books' (see page 178).

This label can cause confusion simply because of the breadth and variety of intentions and outcomes of those held within its catchment. (This ambiguity can also be seen as a virtue: the Fluxus movement made much of the interaction between broad-ranging ideas and methods encouraged by print.) Many even took printing seriously enough to explore and reinvent the technologies of its past as well as developing new and ingenious digital overlaps.

Below:
A mainframe computer being delivered to Norwich City Council's Treasurer's Department, 1957. What is surprising is not only the enormous size and weight of the computer but also the elementary means at hand to manoeuvre it from the lorry and through the door of the building.

Below right:
Nam June Paik, *Robot K-456*, exhibited in *Cybernetic Serendipity*, ICA Gallery, London, 1968. Described in the catalogue as 'a female robot known for her disturbing and idiosyncratic behaviour'.

Opposite page:
The Boeing Computer Graphics organisation, c. 1968. A computer-generated image from a project concerned with the ergonomic layout of an aircraft cockpit. The computer used was an IBM 7094 with Gerber plotter, and an IBM 1400C reader printer.

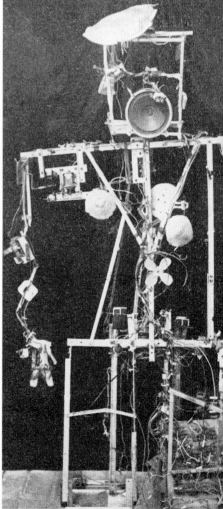

Chapter 5:
Inevitability of digital technology

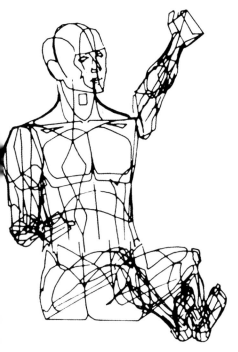

The computer

During the 18th century, people employed by the Royal Observatory in London to make repeated calculations were called 'computers'. Between 1870 and 1940 a number of analogue 'computing' machines were invented to improve the accuracy and speed of similar calculations. These machines generally replicated a physical phenomenon by mechanical or electrical means. For example, one of earliest was a tidal predictor in which an arrangement of wheels and pulleys produced a graph showing the sea level to be expected at a given place at a given time. Such a machine had one specific problem to solve. It was during the first part of the 20th century, culminating with the Second World War, that Alan Turing demonstrated the possibility of building a single electronic 'universal computing machine' that could do *anything*.

Commercially constructed computers began to appear in their huge mainframe form in the 1950s, usually filling specially built rooms in government departments and universities. Initially, users did not usually have direct contact with the machine, but instead would prepare tasks for the computer elsewhere on other equipment, for example, in the form of punch cards, which were delivered and collected by hand. Given tasks might take hours or even days.

The mechanical complexity of these mainframe computers was a cause for frustration as much as wonderment. In the UK, Norwich City Council's first computer was delivered to the City Treasurer's Department in 1957. Considering it had almost 3,000 plugs and sockets it is not surprising that the time between failures averaged just twelve hours. Nevertheless, just eleven years later, the creative potential of similar 'monster computers' was being celebrated in hugely influential exhibition, *Cybernetic Serendipity*, held at the ICA Gallery, London, 1968.

From the beginning, computers were promoted as being capable of negating the need for paper. Information, it was claimed, could not only be stored but also retrieved more efficiently on, for example, punch cards, punched tape,[48] microfilm[49] and hard disks. The smaller, lighter, soft or 'floppy' disks became available in 1971.

The feasibility of the paperless office was presented in a *Business Week* article in 1975 in which it was suggested that office automation would make paper redundant for basic tasks such as record-keeping and book keeping.[50] George E Pake, who was then head of the Xerox Corporation's Palo Alto Research Center (PARC) is quoted in the article saying that in twenty years time his office will be very different; most important being the TV-display terminal with keyboard sitting on his desk. 'I'll be able to call up documents from my files on the screen, or by pressing a button,' he said, 'I can get my mail or any messages. I don't know how much hard copy [printed paper] I'll want in this world.'

The 'paperless' concept became a great deal more prevalent with the introduction of the personal computer and was promoted vigorously as a key advantage of computer technology for business. The idea of decluttering the office by removing the need for paper – fast becoming a symbol of old-fashioned practices and old-fashioned technology – proved to be an effective way of exalting the advantage of this new technology to a conservative business community. But while Pake's

Opposite page, left:
Advertisement for the Picturephone, 'a product of the future' that Western Electric, USA, claimed to be developing during the 1950s. Why, the advert asks, use paper and ink when you can talk?

Opposite page, right:
Cover of the catalogue *Cybernetic Serendipity: the Computer and the Arts*, an exhibition held at the ICA Gallery, London, 1968. *(Designer not credited.)*

Below:
Shot Kennedy Number 1, Fujio Niwa, and *Diffused Kennedy*, Massao Komura, The Computer Technique Group (CTG) working at the IBM Scientific Data Centre, Tokyo 1967–68. Data from a photograph is converted into straight lines converging at one point at the ear. The deformation programme can be applied to any pattern. The synthesis of emotive response and computer technology was a major theme of *Cybernetic Serendipity*. From the exhibition catalogue, 1968.

prediction of a personal computer (or 'TV-display terminal') on every desk proved correct, the 'paperless office' did not.

Computer screens became landscape-orientated, capable of displaying two 'pages' side-by-side and linked to other computers with the same configuration. What else was this connection for other than to send and receive documents? And what else was the desktop computer for but composing those documents and storing them in virtual 'folders' within virtual 'cabinets'. And yet, to everyone's amazement, and despite the sale of millions of computers, the use of paper in commercial offices continued to grow.

In fact, paper played a significant role in spreading knowledge and general interest in computer technology. The voluminous manuals that accompanied computers and software purchases were (and remain) notoriously difficult to navigate and before the Internet there was a desperate need for user-friendly, illustrated magazines that would focus on, for example, a specific computer or operating system, software category, or software application. By 1983, the *New York Times* reported the number of computer magazines being published at that time to be more than 200 (not including 'new media' magazines being published on floppy disks). Such a phenomenon remains unprecedented in the history of magazine publishing.

The Internet and hypertext

The 19th century telegraph was the first, if elemental, digital communication system and 20th century early mainframe computers used the same point-to-point communication technology to link them with terminals elsewhere. However, this form of communication was compromised because the necessary *physical* link was deemed inherently unsafe for strategic and military use because there were no alternative paths of communication if the line were cut.

The World Wide Web was created by the British scientist Tim Berners-Lee using a NeXT computer (see page 95) at CERN during the second half of 1990.[51] Networks were established, initially between academic libraries and science departments, but these quickly grew in size and distance. Others followed and the potential of a global network was quickly recognised if the existing separate physical networks could themselves be merged to form a single international network, or 'internet'. By the mid 1990s the Internet had become a fully functioning, fully democratic, worldwide information-sharing medium and the commercial potential of its 'connectibility' was quickly recognised.

Entrepreneurs stalked the Internet looking for viable economic models. Free services supported by advertising, such as those offering chat rooms or message boards for community building, was a typical early strategy. However, direct online sales grew as companies and web designers ('graphic' designers by another name) adapted the technology to give customers the necessary information they needed and a trustworthy payment process in order to make a purchase. Some products – books, for example – proved particularly easy to sell online (efficient to store, pack and send by post). A basic knowledge of the subject or of an author's work, also makes them a minimum-risk online purchase. But it is not only the buying of books that has been dramatically influenced by the Internet, so has reading and writing.

Nothing demonstrates the astonishing, free-flowing and liberating aspect of the World Wide Web than hypertext. Here is an innovation that offered a genuine alternative to print, and something that could not be replicated by print.

The concept of hypertext had been described by Vannevar Bush in his article 'As We May Think', for *The Atlantic*, July 1945, in which he explained Memex, a machine with which individuals would compress and store all of their books, records, and communications whilst also enabling speedy and flexible access.[52] The concept of the memex influenced the development of early hypertext systems and of personal knowledge based software. But it took another thirty years for hypertext to become a reality – there could not be hypertext without efficient computers and the Internet.

It has been argued that whilst hypertext gives the reader more control it also places responsibility for the actual narrative and/or the process of information-gathering firmly in the reader's hands and so relegates the status of the author. For someone seeking to understand an idea or theory the learner must now monitor to a greater extent whether he or she understands what has been read, determine whether information must be sought to close information gaps, and decide where to look for that information in the text. In short, there are greater metacognitive demands on the reader during hypertext-assisted learning.[53]

Below:
The map of *Victory Garden*, a novel by Stuart Moulthrop (1991). This map or 'network' represents only the top layer of the text's structure: each signpost on the map represents a region of the text that contains a further system of links.

For example, hypertext might encourage a student to flit from document to document when it might be better to stick to a recommended author's structured argument. But such decisions will be part of a broader learning process and if used appropriately the flexibility of hypertext can be positive. It has been argued that '...electronic writing space gives [works from the past] a new "typography." Hypertext is the typography of the electronic medium.'[54]

The creative potential of hypertext for the author became a major topic during the 1990s. Robert Coover in his essay, 'The End of Books', explored this new multi-layered, multimedia-based, and seemingly infinite non-sequential narrative space provided by hypertext. Surely this new and dynamic story-telling medium would supplant, or at the very least diminish, the fixed, finite, sequential and non-negotiable structure of books?

In another essay titled, 'Hyperfiction: Novels for the Computer', Coover focused on the hypertext novel *Victory Garden*, by Stuart Moulthrop, 1993. His essay was published on the front page of the *New York Times Book Review*[55] and in it he provided a description of what hyperfiction entailed for the reader:

> The routes through Stuart Moulthrop's new hyperfiction *Victory Garden* are almost literally countless. Altogether there are nearly a thousand text spaces and over 2,800 electronic links between them. One is invited to 'come in' by way of a sentence constructed by the reader, word by word, out of a set of choices that will yield as many as fifty-six different such sentences on the themes of beginnings, labyrinths, time, America, words, dreams, truth. When completed, these opening sentences link to at least forty-seven different starting points in the narrative proper, from which there are no fewer than 194 separate links to other text spaces, each in turn with branching options.

The idea that literature could mimic real life; where narratives evolve as a result of a myriad of seemingly arbitrary choices: dynamic, unpredictable and entirely free of authorial trajection, was ground-breaking. (The Italian Futurist, Marinetti, would surely have been an enthusiast!) So why didn't it transform and transport story-telling into what some in the 1990s were confidently heralding 'the post-Gutenberg era'?

Perhaps it is that readers are reluctant to start something that cannot be finished, or, more mundanely, it might be that the constant 'clicking' on highlighted words and then waiting for the connected text to appear became, finally, just too tedious to continue (Nancy Princenthal, in *The American Book Review,* compared jumping about in hypertext to 'late-night channel surfing: empowering, perhaps, but not altogether satisfying'). It appears that readers prefer to experience the ebb and flow of a narrative that depends on the imagination of a chosen author, rather than their own. And even more mundanely, there is the vexing issue of ever-evolving software. I have a copy of *Victory Garden* but I can't read it any more because, so my computer informs me, 'the classic environment is no longer supported'.

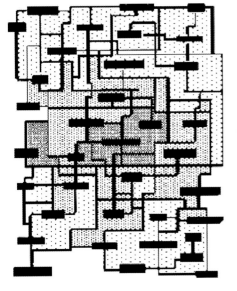

Below:
Books in supermarkets represent a significant percentage of over-all book sales although what such stores generally offer is little more than the 'top-fifty' bestsellers.

Opposite page:
The Shakespeare and Company bookshop, Paris. Small-scale events such as this are a regular feature, in this case the author (left) is French novelist Frédéri. The original shop was opened by Sylvia Beach, an American, in 1919, and became a gathering place for many young aspiring writers such as Ezra Pound, Ernest Hemingway, and James Joyce. It closed in 1941 during the German occupation.

The second and current bookstore is situated at 37 rue de la Bûcherie. Photograph by David Grove.

Paper publishing's crisis of confidence

Amazon, the global Internet superstore, was founded in 1994. Jeff Bezos, its Chief Executive Officer, considered calling the company Relentless.com before finally adopting the name of the world's largest river by volume. It was not a love of books that caused Bezos to establish an online bookstore but rather their inherent physical attributes: books are easy to pack and hard to break.[56] Crucially, he also noted that there are far too many books for any single physical store to hold even a tiny fraction of them (and this was the time of the vast 'big box bookstores' of Borders and Barns & Noble). The accessibility and vast selection of books made possible by the Internet gave Amazon its advantage, and, once established, enabled it to begin selling everything else. For Bezos to have recognised that an online bookstore was the means to world commercial domination when the publishing world was in a state of crisis was a masterstroke.

Publishing's crisis of confidence was due to the giants of mass-merchandising, such as Walmart and Tesco, taking an increasing amount of the book market by stocking just the best-selling volumes and selling them at discounted prices. This strategy was so successful that they sold more books than the specialist 'big box' book shops such as Barnes & Noble and Borders combined, who in turn had caused

the closure of numerous small, characterful independent bookshops. The worry for publishers was that enterprises such as Walmart, could decide to reduce or even eliminate the space they devote to books at a moment's notice. Michael Norris, editor of the *Book Publishing Report*, explained, 'Walmart wouldn't hesitate to rid their stores of books if it meant replacing them with higher margin items. [...] In a bookstore, the future of the store depends on books. In a non-bookstore, the future of the book depends on the store.'[57]

Below:
Jeff Bozos, Chief Executive Officer of Amazon, stated that, 'To do something like [Amazon's Kindle] you have to be as good as the paper and ink book'. But the arbitary 'setting' of the text, especially the resultant large and variously sized gaps between words, demonstrates how far short of the printed book the on-screen reading experience remains.

When Amazon became established, publishers everywhere suddenly had a new buyer that was dependable, paid quickly and, uniquely, displayed and sold the whole of their backlist as well as new titles. Publishers were not concerned that Amazon sold their books at huge discounts (that was the independent bookshop's problem, not theirs) in fact, they were keen to collaborate and even used Amazon as an information resource.

By the turn of the 21st century Bezos, having seen Apple dominate the music-selling business with iTunes and the iPod, was determined that the same would not happen with books. In 2004, he set up a laboratory in Silicon Valley to design and build Amazon's first consumer hardware and in 2007, Bezos unveiled the Kindle. This was not, by any means, the first electronic-book reader, but with Amazon's financial backing, it established the e-book as a substantial threat to the paper-and-ink book.

The e-book

The first e-book had been produced on the fourth of July, 1971 when Michael Hart, then a student at the University of Illinois, typed the text of the United States Declaration of Independence into a computer network to which he and about one hundred others had access. Project Gutenberg was born. Over the next two decades many more texts were added by Hart and other volunteers, the aim being to create a database providing (in plain ASCII) free access to out-of-copyright texts or texts offered by authors. More recently, texts have also been made available in HTML, PDF, EPUB, MOBI, and Plucker (for Palm OS). The Project Gutenberg website established its current form in 1991 and a target was set to add one book each month. Today, hundreds of books are added monthly.

The organisation has retained a bohemian aspect to its cause that reflects something of early 1970s attitudes. It is still run by volunteers, its website carries no advertising and there are no extraneous marketing ploys such as 'book of the day', or 'author of the week', etc. There is an equally relaxed attitude to the selection of texts, the criteria being that if someone thinks a book worthy of the effort to retype, or in recent years, scan, then it will be included.

Meanwhile, there have been several generations of dedicated hardware e-readers. The Rocket eBook and several others were introduced toward the end of the 1990s, but did not gain widespread acceptance. The establishment of the E Ink Corporation led to the development of electronic paper, a technology which allows a display screen to reflect light in the same way as paper and so eliminated the need for a backlight. Electronic paper was incorporated first into the Sony Librie, released in 2004, and then the Sony Reader, 2006.

When, in the following year, Amazon released the Kindle it was a momentous occasion. Amazon's close association with printed books gave the Kindle a unique viability. This was backed up by a general lack of 'hyperbole' accompanying its release. For example, and understandably, there were no strident 'end of print' forecasts as had been the case with previous other electronic readers. Instead, the Kindle was promoted as an *extension* of the printed book. Bezos was reported saying, 'If you're going to do something like this, you have to be as good as the [paper and ink] book in a lot of respects. But we also have to look for things that ordinary books can't do.'[58]

'Things' such as the ability to search within the book for a phrase or name, or to change the size of the font, were lauded. Its 'bookish' characteristics included its size and its weight – about ten ounces or 290 grams, and a similar size to a paperback – and silent when working. However, for Bezos, the Kindle was always intended to be less of a book and more a bookshop. In fact, it was an extension of the familiar Amazon online store, effectively a shop window for Amazon.com from which to view and buy more e-books (or even paper and ink books). Naturally, buying a book from Amazon with a Kindle was, and is, very easy, as Bezos boasted, 'The vision is that you should be able to buy and get any book on this device in less than a minute'.

Like everyone else, Bezos was watching Apple, his main concern being that it might have ambitions to take over book selling in the same way it had come to dominate the music-selling business. He was right. The iPad, launched by Apple in April 2010, was a 'tablet' computer that simply came with an optional free iBooks application enabling books, magazines and newspapers to be bought and downloaded from the newly created online iBookstore (with publishers, including Harper Collins, Penguin, Simon & Schuster, Macmillan and the Hachette Book Group happily providing the content). With Apple having successfully reduced the size of their computers to the size of an A4 sheet of paper or less, it was inevitable that devices such as the Kindle, designed primarily for reading purposes, would quickly become passé.

The development period of the iPad had been some twenty-one years and just how much digital technology had changed during that time is clear from an account given by Tom Dair, co-founder and president of Smart Design. In 1989 his company was commissioned by Apple to develop a design concept for a tablet device. The two-page project brief [59] included a line drawing of a rectangular slab form with a few basic dimensions, an indication of the screen size and approximate weight. Apple asked for the delivery of two designs in the form of non-working appearance models and five images of each design to demonstrate how people would use them.

Smart Design duly worked up two concepts, one suggesting that the case would be made from aluminium with precisely machined holes for the speakers and a slit-like opening on the top surface into which a (credit card size) memory card, required for the storage of applications and files, could be inserted. It also included 'a high quality lens positioned on the top edge [that] would allow people to capture images for direct viewing on the screen. [...] To protect the screen and to give the tablet a

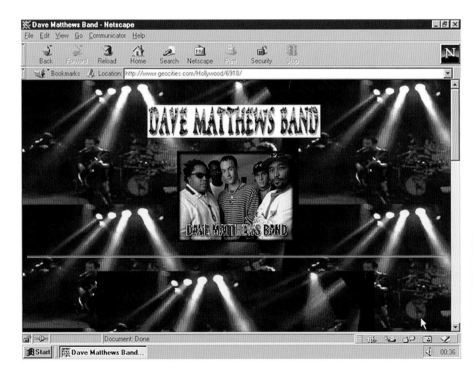

folio/briefcase appearance, a brown leather cover was added. The cover was secured closed with magnets and a handy loop was sewn in to hold a bone-like stylus in place during transit.' The models were packed up and dispatched and, 'after that, we never heard another word from them'. Neither, apparently, did the other three companies commissioned by Apple.

Four years later Apple released its first foray into tablet computing in 1993, the Newton MessagePad, Apple's first touchscreen device. Weighing just one pound (0.45 kilogram) the Newton paved the way for future innovations in mobile technology and the iPad in particular: a computer (albeit with limited scope) designed specifically to access media. For the first time, books, journals and newspapers could now be accessed in much the same way as Apple had already established for video and music.

Websites

The year after Tim Berners-Lee wrote the first web browser he published the first website, a single page that explained the elemental features of the Web: how to access other people's documents and how to set up your own server. Initial versions of HTML (Hypertext Markup Language) only allowed for very basic content structure: headings, paragraphs and links. Later versions allowed the addition of images to pages, whilst 'tables', intended to enable tabular data to be shown, was adopted by designers to provide a grid-like structure with which textual material could be organised.

Developed in 1996, Cascading Style Sheets (css) enabled the separation of document content from document presentation, including aspects such as the typographic arrangement, colours, and fonts. Invented by Håkon Wium Lie, css is similar in principle to 'style sheets' found in DTP software. css encourages consistency of style by enabling multiple HTML pages to share the same formatting specifications. This meant that all headings, subheadings and textual material spread over numerous pages could be amended by simply changing the specification on the relevant style sheet.

As the 1990s progressed, the appearance and performance of websites was driven by the technology, with the result that 'change' became 'enhancement' and so colour-changing navigations, tiled background images, clashing colours, 3D buttons all became common features. Garish and fractured, irrelevant and pointlessly time-consuming, website design in the late 1990s hit a new low point. Form and function had become, briefly, two entirely unrelated trains of thought. Flash software, designed by a small design company called FutureWave, was a major influence in enabling this[60] and for a period, attraction was certainly given precedence over functionality. But it was eventually realised that by doing this many sites had become for viewers, quite literally, 'one-hit' wonders.

As the Internet moved towards the goal of being a truly global network of net-works, commercial enterprises realised that a Web presence was essential. In its first few years, the benefits of access to information worldwide and free publishing was appreciated, but it was also clear to the business community that mass social familiarity with two-way communication over an international network offered huge potential for Web-based commerce (or e-commerce). Dotcom companies proliferated, especially between 1997 and 2000 – leading to one of the biggest economic booms in history.

It was a new and innovative industry with huge potential, but also one in which companies were difficult to value. Investors, in a state of 'irrational exuberance'[61] and apparently dazzled by the unfathomable, dismissed the reality represented by elemental arithmetic and, instead, invested huge amounts of money into the newest and most implausible digital concepts. The result was disaster. Beginning 11th March 2000, dotcoms were suddenly renamed 'dotbombs' when the Nasdaq went into a free fall as investors began to realise *en-masse* that most of the loss-making new-tech companies were, indeed, nothing more than loss-making tech companies.

Perhaps as a result, a more intelligent view of design for digital technology now took precedence. It was at this time that developments began to move toward what might be called the modern web: the growth of multimedia applications, the implementation of easier and more purposeful interactive content, and the phenomenal rise of the social web – all of which had been part of Berners-Lee's original vision. Moreover, these features began to dictate the way web design was approached. Design was, at last, being led by content not technology, and the content was being written and organised to optimise the ability of interested viewers to find the site and, having arrived, the focus became accessibility, adaptability and usability.[62] Aesthetic changes, including flat simpler layouts (no 3D buttons!); simpler architecture, such as infinite scrolling; more subtle use of colour (although these continue to be distorted by different browsers and user hardware); increased and much improved creative use of photography, and greater attention to typography, albeit still requiring major compromises between performance, support and desired deliver of presentation. For the web designer, the only way to maintain any semblance of sanity was, apparently, to continue deceiving themselves that 'perfection is overrated'.[63]

The web designer's task had little to commend it. The result of attempting to reduce the worst effects of not having total control is that on-screen textual communication gravitates toward a similar limited pool of reliable resolutions. For a site visitor this means the reading experience will lack distinction. But if simply getting information out to the widest possible audience is the main – perhaps sole – priority, then the value of the Web is explained in this excerpt from the Opera Web Standards Curriculum, written by Paul Haine in 2014:

> This lack of control needn't be a problem – you just have to get used to the idea that people will want to read your content on a variety of devices in a variety of environments in a variety of ways. You shouldn't try to stop them, or make it difficult for them – if they want to read your content then it should be as easy to do so as possible. They may wish to read it on their mobile device during their commute home; they may prefer to print everything out and read it on paper instead of a screen; they may be visually impaired and need to increase the font

size somewhat. This is why, when you style your text on the Web, what you're really doing is providing a guide to all the different browsing devices as to how you'd prefer that text be seen. Devices are free to ignore everything you say, of course, but that's okay – what matters is that you're not trying to force your design decisions on your entire audience.'

The lack of typographic control for the designer and the subsequent diminishment of the reading experience on the Web will be resolved over time, but it is a deficiency that becomes increasingly evident as other operational standards continue to advance. With the aid of software improvements and more powerful hardware, websites have made another leap forward, although 'forward' in this case is demonstrated by the growing ability – and stated preference – to look and behave evermore like print.

For website designers, the allure of print was previously something that not only had to be denied but condemned, the oft-repeated reason being that a new era is best reflected by new media. Yet since 2010, the allure of print has been rediscovered and conspicuously mimicked by digital media.[64] Perhaps this renewed print ethos will be the impetus for software developers to concentrate on providing greater typographic control for the web designer. Web fonts, for example, that enable web designers to use – and viewers to see – any font even if not installed on the viewer's computer. Unfortunately such developments are currently stalled due to licensing issues. However, the reacceptance of print as the standard is surely also a capitulation and acceptance that the screen, in all its formats, and regardless of resolution factors, remains second best to the physical diversity and creative opportunities that is offered by print.

New symbiotic relationships

Wired is a magazine whose *raison d'etre* is to be closely aligned to the development of digital technology, critically reviewing and commenting on emerging technologies and how they affect culture, the economy and politics. In 2015 the company redesigned its online version of *Wired* magazine in a conscious effort to make it look and function more like its printed version: same typeface, full-page section images, close alignment with contents and feature pages as well as an editorial orientation around business, design, entertainment, hardware, etc.

After all the entrepreneurial optimism, media hyperbole, and millions of dollars invested in a celebrated digital alternative, print remains the 'standard' for reading matter, whilst electronic alternatives are perceived as copies of the genuine article. The holy grail of the digital era, now that the revolutionary fervour has dissipated, is to find the means of replicating the look and feel of printed paper. As early as 2002, Abigail Sellen and Richard Harper, in their book *The Myth of the Paperless Office*, were already anticipating this ideal: 'What has spurred this new wave of hope is the fact that [digital] technologies are beginning to look and feel more paper-like.'[65] Some thirteen years later, when *Wired* explained the reasoned economic, aesthetic and business sense of redesigning its online magazine to resemble the appearance

Opposite page:
An Amazon warehouse. Few products are more
efficient to store, pack and post than books.

of its celebrated printed version it was described as a 'turning point' for digital
technology.[66] It was agreed that new levels of visual sophistication was now being
achieved on-screen, but it was also the moment when a major arbiter of new
technologies accepted that, in fact, digital tools were destined to mimic print.

What does this mean for a technology that was once predicted to be 'the death
of print'? Revues of the 'new' online *Wired* were complimentary but, unusually for
the new-media press, the language was less strident, even subdued. Opinion was
diplomatically summed up by American publication designer Roger Black, who
commented, 'I don't think of this as making digital publications look like print.
It's more a case of making them look right – and readable.'

In other words, to 'look right' and function correctly (to be 'readable') print
provides the standard. This is not surprising. For well over 500 years printers and
then graphic designers have fine-tuned the art of printed typography to function
in the myriad ways that their customers have devised for its use. Digital technology
delivers information in a very different way to print, but it still uses words that the
recipient is required to read if communication is to take place. And yet, swept up in
the rhetoric of a 'communication revolution', it was loudly trumpeted that digital
technology changed everything. For a brief period it seemed that graphic design and
typography would have to be essentially relearnt: *Emigre* magazine's 'Starting from
Zero' issue in 1991 was dedicated to this 'primary process'.[67]

Some twenty-five years later, and a more rational view has come to the fore, one
in which a growing symbiotic relationship enables pixels and paper to function side
by side. Publishers of other iconic printed magazines, such as *Vogue* and *New Yorker*,
etc, have also (but without the trumpets) been carefully adjusting their online
presence as technology and software allowed, to appear and function in much the
same way as their celebrated printed versions. Meanwhile, Jeff Bezos has positioned
Amazon to gain from the best qualities of both digital and print technology.

Below:

Johannes Gutenberg, forty-two-line *Bible*, printed in two volumes in Mainz, c.1455. The most important asset of Gutenberg's invention of printing from individually cast letters was that every comma, letter and word was identical across the whole edition.

However, when we compare different Gutenberg *Bibles* today what is most apparent is how much their appearance differs. Gutenberg left spaces for decorative initials and headings to be added and many owners also commissioned further decorative material. In addition, restorative work has caused pages to be trimmed, changing dimensions as well as overall size.

Opposite page:

Erhard Ratdolt, *Praeclarissimus liber completus in judiciis astrorum* ('The very famous complete book on the judgement of the stars') 1485. Ratdolt is the most celebrated of the German printers to set up his business in 15th century Venice. Printed just thirty-one years after Gutenberg's *Bible*, Ratdolt's typeface was modelled on the formal handwriting style ('Carolingian') used in handwritten books before the invent of printing. All the characteristics we recognise today in a 'book' have been established.

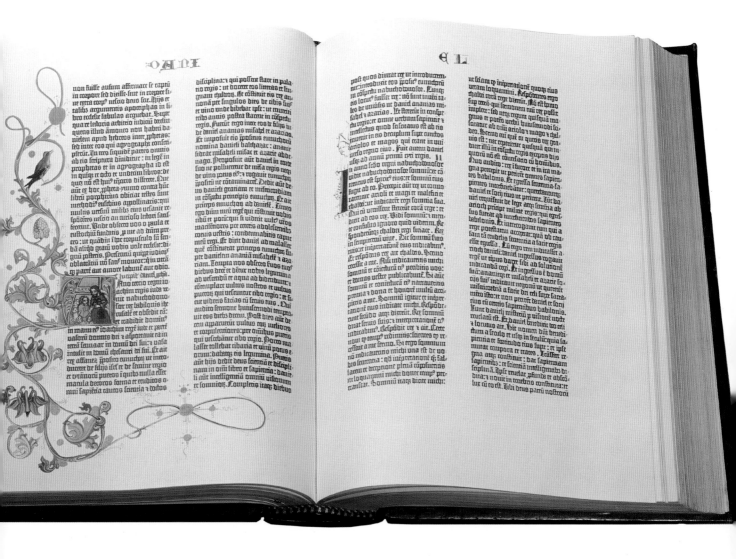

Chapter 6:
The persistence of paper

The advantage of permanence

One of the most valued aspects of Johannes Gutenberg's invention of printing from moveable metal type, c. 1455, was that it guaranteed the content of multiple copies of a book were all precisely the same. Previously, books had been written by hand, each one copied from another previously handwritten book. Mistakes were inevitable and as each copy was made existing mistakes could be included – and new ones added.

Nevertheless, such books were treasured, not only for the wisdom they contained (with or without errors) but also because they were rare and expensive. They were also, sometimes, extremely beautiful. But by the end of the 15th century the Renaissance was at its height and universities were being established all over Europe. Students needed books with which they could study, discuss and compare notes with their peers. The printing press gave them consistency and in so doing helped validate the content of the book. Books printed and published in Venice by Erhard Ratdolt, Nicolas Jenson, Aldus Manutius, Christoph Plantin and others were admired because these were also scholars who took great pains to find original sources and hired the expertise of other specialist scholars to check and ensure their books were accurate.

Printed books encouraged scholars to argue about the accuracy and interpretations of texts. And where errors were discovered, following editions were corrected, a transparent process that added to the level of trust in print. It was due to the efforts of these early scholar-printers – who were also remarkable craftsmen – that the 'book' came to represent the authoritative 'fount of knowledge' it has retained to this day. The fact that such knowledge, having been set down could then be precisely repeated, was greatly valued and established a level of trust in the book unlikely before Gutenberg.

Gutenberg printed between 160 and 185 copies of his two-volume *Bible*, but the intrinsic stability of print on paper or vellum has proved that, fire and water apart, books have a remarkable capacity to survive (forty-eight copies, or substantial portions, of Gutenberg's *Bible* remain today). Survival rates are improved by the fact that copies of such an edition are often distributed all around the world and held in different circumstances – private owners, libraries, museums – an ideal strategy for the preservation of any multiple publication. The oldest known surviving (woodblock)

Below:
The British Library, 2016. Visitors write up their research on laptops. The British Library has provided additional tables and digital work stations in and around the coffee areas in 2016 in response to the increasing demand for access to its collection.

printed book, the *Diamond Sūtra*[68] was discovered hidden in a sealed-up cave in north-west China in 1907. It had laid there for well over 1,000 years. Yet although made in the year 868 this is not the earliest example of a printed book, but it is the oldest, so far, to be found bearing a date.

Perversely, it is the high survival rate of print that was part of the argument for the promotion of digital technology. Storage of books and other printed material, especially in the light of current exponential rates of production, certainly provides major problems. For example, as a legal deposit library,[69] the British Library receives copies of all books, magazines and newspapers produced in the United Kingdom and Ireland, and also a significant proportion of overseas titles distributed in the UK. These add up to around three million items requiring an estimated six miles (9.6 kilometres) of new shelf space annually.

The storage culture

'Casual' printing and data storage in the offices of commercial enterprises have developed a print culture all its own, and quite separate from the print and publishing trades. In these systemised environments typewriting, duplicating, storage and retrieval practices were all interlinked.

Marshall McLuhan in his book, *The Gutenberg Galaxy*, 1962, discussed at length the changing media environment caused by an 'electronic world' that was calling into question previous certainties: 'Our most ordinary and conventional attitudes seem suddenly twisted into gargoyles and grotesques. Familiar institutions and associations seem at times menacing and malignant'.[70] Companies such as Gestetner and Roneo made every effort to consolidate these changes by expanding their range of products to affirm their hold on information storage markets, creating specially designed office, library and banking equipment. In the 1970s, Roneo developed automated filing and data retrieval systems to organise and store millions of correspondence files. These were marketed as being the 'scientific' solution for modern management procedures before the computer. Systems were sold to national and academic libraries and, in this way, imposed a commercial attitude to order onto scholarship through modular containers on modular shelving in modular-framed buildings. Previous common ad-hoc systems such as the 'spike' (a nail on which business correspondence was impaled) were, understandably, deemed archaic.

Although archived physical documents provide a huge amount of information beyond their printed textual content, it is often the case that a researcher will only need to access the text itself. But when the text is printed on low-grade material, such as a newspaper, it might be the case that to read is also to cause irreparable damage. In the 1980s and 1990s many libraries adopted a policy of copying newspaper content on to microfilm, after which they destroyed what was left of the original.

The novelist Nicholas Baker in his book *Double Fold: Libraries and the Assault on Paper*, 2001, attacked this 'wonton destruction of the material record' since newspapers had to be cut in order to be recorded. But although Baker and other's protests prompted an important debate at a point when digital archiving was gathering pace, it is important to recognise the archivist's formidable task of dealing with a collection of printed culture that continues to grow. Every archive has corners in which printed ephemera has gathered in a pathetic state: already frayed, torn, dusty, discoloured, and all too often folded and compressed into unwieldy bundles by previous owners. Anyone who has had the opportunity to wander behind the scenes of a large archive will find it hard to imagine how anyone with sufficient expertise will ever be given the time to disentangle, repair and catalogue such material. Indeed, maintaining control and accessibility to an unending volume of print must appear, at best, daunting, and an impossibility at any other time. For some, making digital copies offered an answer.

Digitising print archives

Having a digital record of printed matter would save huge amounts of space, although this assumes that the original paper-based material would then be dispensed with – together with their expensive buildings and restoration programmes. But in the very brief time that digital technology has been in existence, its functional and physical state has been one of constant change, sometimes motivated by technical improvements, but *always* by commercial imperatives. Managed obsolescence is a critical part of any manufacturing company's longer-term strategy and for the digital media user this means that access to digital content will be compromised when 'external dependencies' – be that hardware, software or other physical carriers – are no longer manufactured. This means that, for example, a laptop computer lasts, on average, just four years before it needs to be 'upgraded'.

As a result, digitally stored material must be copied from one storage system to the next 'updated' version in order to ensure material remains accessible. Lev Manovich, in *The Language of New Media*, talking about film archives describes the situation like this: 'Since the 1960s the operation of media translation has been at the core of our culture. Films transferred to video, then transferred from one video format to another, video transferred to digital data, digital data transferred from one format to another – from floppy disk to Jaz drives, from CD-Rom to DVDs, and so on indefinitely.' [71]

Many libraries with major collections of printed matter, be it books, journals, posters and other ephemera, have set about digitising the more important examples from their collections in a bid to make them accessible via the Internet. But issues regarding technical obsolescence are causing many to question the long-term value of committing to a programme of digitising whole collections and, instead, are tending to concentrate their efforts on maintaining only popular or exceptional items to be available via their websites.

In the midst of such problems, the breathtaking ambition of Google Books – nothing less than the creation of a cross-referenced universal library that contains every book in existence – dramatically projected a renewed sense of authority on to digital technology. The concept of making every book ever printed (or at least that

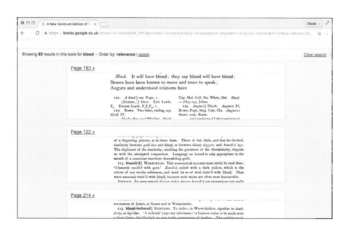

is still in existence somewhere) accessible to everyone is extraordinary and would be considered an impossible objective were it any other company. However, the ubiquity of Google, its global reach and almost unlimited funds, caused the launch in 2004 of Google Books to be met with optimism, if also quizzical restraint. Could this really be possible, even for Google?

When browsing a book in Google Books the user is allowed to view a sequence of whole pages in which the entered search word, name or term appears, as long as the book is out of copyright or if the copyright owner has given permission. If the book is still under copyright, then the user is limited to viewing 'snippets' of text – perhaps three or four lines only – around the highlighted search item. Crucially, no book can be accessed in its entirety.

Google set about this task by reaching an initial agreement with twenty-nine major research libraries including, for example, Harvard University, Oxford University and the New York Public Library, to digitise current and out-of-print books. Approximately twenty-five million books had been scanned to date (there are estimated to be about 130 million books worldwide – and growing, of course). The scale of the project is illustrated by the fact that even Google Books concedes it will take all of the 21st century to complete the task. However, John P Wilkin, associate university librarian at the University of Michigan recently said, 'Our program is strong, and we have been able to digitize approximately 5,000 volumes a year; nevertheless, at this rate, it would take us more than a thousand years to digitize our entire collection.'[72]

There is also the issue of what is suitable for scanning. Libraries will only allow those books which, in the judgement of their own conservationists, will not be adversely affected by the process. All of the libraries in the project have many rare and rather fragile books and it is only natural that they will err on the side of caution and choose books that are in a physically robust condition to be scanned first. The likelihood is that many thousands of the world's rarer books will never, in fact, be part of Google Books. But of greater concern are increasing doubts about Google's ability to sustain long-term interest in the project. As several participating archivists have explained recently, Google themselves are no longer placing the same priority on the books project as they once were – 'they have the funds, but their interest moves on quite rapidly!'[73]

The digital scanning of books presents immense advantages by widening access to rare books and documents, but there is a fundamental problem. Recast as a two-dimensional image, stripped of its physical and material characteristics and scaled to a uniform size, it is impossible for the viewer to properly understand what is represented on screen. Magnification, colour adjustment, page turning software and other screen facilities cannot alter this. And as use of Google Books' database of images increases, so the proportion of people with experience of handling older original material will decline.

Archiving digital material

Since the late 1990s, the British Library has been acquiring an increasing amount of 'born digital' content, ranging from digital audio/video recordings, to personal digital archives, e-journals and archived websites. In 2013 the Library already had more than 11,500,000 items stored in their long-term digital library system, with more awaiting inclusion. With the establishment of non-print legal deposit legislation in 2013, the British Library's annual digital acquisitions will vastly increase. The estimated size of the digital collection by 2020 will be five petabytes (five million gigabytes).[74]

There are three significant issues to be considered when archiving digital material. Firstly, the degrading of digital material and the fragility of digital content means that preservation actions need to be made far earlier (and, therefore, more frequently) than for paper-based collections, advisedly every two years for as long as the information held is deemed to be of value.

Second, there is the issue of securing the integrity of digital material. For instance, it is easier for someone to make unnoticed (even unintentional) changes to digital files than to paper-based material. But it is also necessary for archival staff to adapt commands or structural parameters in order to manage and ensure access is maintained as hardware technology progresses. For a viewer using contemporary equipment to see and use a website as it was designed to be used, for example, a decade earlier, is a challenge, perhaps already impossible.[75] Meanwhile, malicious alteration must be prevented and non-malicious intervention tightly controlled.

Lastly, the media on which digital materials are stored is unstable and its reliability quickly diminishes. This can be made worse by unsuitable storage conditions and handling. The resulting 'bit rot' (or 'data rot', 'data decay', 'data degradation') can prevent files from rendering correctly, if at all. When this happens there is no prior warning and this can occur within just a few years, sometimes less, of the storage carrier having been produced.

Digital preservation is thus not just a technical challenge, it requires a commitment to a never-ending set of procedures if access is to be maintained. In its report, *Digital Preservation Strategy* (March 2013) the British Library summed up the problems as follows:

> Action and intervention is required from before even the point of acquisition, in order to properly manage the risks involved in maintaining digital content for the long term. Only through a comprehensive life-cycle approach can these risks be addressed in a consistent and controlled manner. Furthermore, the strategies we implement must be regularly re-assessed: technologies and technical infrastructures will continue to evolve, so preservation solutions may themselves become obsolete if not regularly re-validated in each new technological environ-ment. Only in this way can we ensure that our digital collections remain reliably accessible and authentic for future users in the very long term.

All of this is a reminder that 'immaterial', a commonly used term when describing the nature of digital technology, is a misnomer. Computational technologies and processes are all embedded in, and dependent upon, multiple levels of solid material;

Below right:
This is a screen shot taken from a NeXT computer running Tim Berners-Lee's original interactive World Wide Web browser 1991. It took a long time for technology to make Berners-Lee's original vision a possibility. The first ever web browser was only able to run on the NeXTSTEP operating system.

Below far right:
This screen shot was taken in 1993 from a NeXT computer. There is surprisingly little difference between these windows and the appearance of today's browsers.

processors, servers, networks, silicon, input/output devices. Each of which has an all-too-brief life span.

The issues regarding the preservation of digital material is well illustrated by a current project being undertaken at CERN to restore the world's first website that was developed by Tim Berners-Lee in 1991. Berners-Lee's NeXT computer – the original web server – is still at CERN and as part of the ongoing project CERN reinstated the website to its original address and in this way preserve some of the digital assets (including a recreation of the original hardware encoded typeface) that are associated with the birth of the Web.[76] The original website together with the method of browsing it had 'died' some twenty-three years previously. The current CERN website (as of January 2016) introduces the project thus: 'For a start, we would like to restore the first URL – put back the files that were there at their earliest possible iterations. Then we will look at the first web servers at CERN see what assets from them we can preserve and share. We will also sift through documentation and try to restore machine names and IP addresses to their original state. Beyond this we want to make http://info.cern.ch – the first web address – a destination that reflects the story of the beginnings of the web for the benefit of future generations.'[77]

Perhaps indifference to the preservation of digital history is shaped by the fact that pixels not only have no intrinsic value but also have no physical presence. But there is also the mistaken idea that once a URL (Uniform Resource Locator or 'web address') exists it is there forever. But as Mark Boulton, a member of the team working on the restoration project at CERN explains, 'That's not the case. You can have a URL, but then URL stop working. Just a few days ago quite a well-known magazine in the UK closed its website. All the URL for all the articles from the past 4–5 years are dead. Gone. If you wanted to find an article on that site now, you can't. And that's a problem.'[78]

An example of how fatally capricious the Web can be is demonstrated by the demise of GeoCities, a web hosting service founded in 1994 by David Bohnett and John Rezner. By 1999, GeoCities was the third-most visited website when it was acquired by Yahoo! In its original form, site users of GeoCities selected a 'city' in which to place their website. The 'cities' were named after real cities or regions according to their content; for example, computer-related sites were placed in 'Silicon Valley' whilst those dealing with entertainment were assigned to 'Hollywood'.

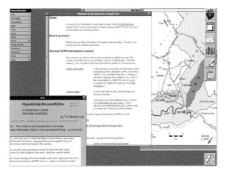
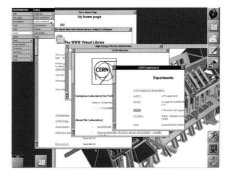

Below right:
A book that shows signs of use is generally the sign of a useful book. This example was already showing signs of heavy use when bought second-hand many years ago but continues to function faultlessly. Published by The Studio Publications Inc, 1955.

Opposite page:
Prior to the 18th century it was common practice for a book collector to have all books re-bound identically. During the Victorian era as books became relatively cheap to produce, publishers grouped an author or genre together and marketed them as 'collections' or 'library series'. Covers were identical (apart from title and author) to mimic the appearance of the great private collections and encourage the 'common man' to build an 'esteemed' literary collection of his own.

Shortly after its acquisition by Yahoo! this practice was abandoned in favour of using the Yahoo! member names in the URLS.

Ten years after Yahoo! bought GeoCities, the company announced that it would shut down the United States GeoCities service on 26 October 2009. There were at least 38 million user-built pages on GeoCities before it was shut down. All that remains today is the GeoCities Japan version of the service – but only in Japanese.[79]

The most valued aspects of digital technology has always been its immediacy and, therefore, transitory nature. Whilst print generally represents a definitive version, digital is a relentless ongoing process, capable of being edited, adjusted, taken down and resurrected minute by minute as deemed necessary. These activities remind the user of its sustained incompleteness and constant state of change. Indeed, this is the point and the daily business of digital communication. Archiving an annual 'snapshot' of websites, blogs etc will not provide a true record of the way digital technology is used, or even a true record of its content.

Compare this to the archiving of paper-based material – itself not without difficulties. Different papers degrade at varying speeds, newsprint being the worst culprit, but most paper-based material can still be handled hundreds of years after being printed. Importantly, paper degrades at a relatively predictable rate and so if damage or deterioration is discovered there is still time to analyse the problem, make plans and have repairs or restorative action take place. The most vulnerable part of a book or a journal is its binding and the most common cause of damage occurs when it is forcibly opened flat – unavoidable when content is scanned for digital records.

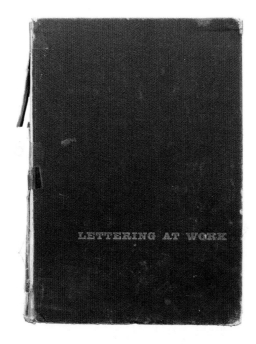
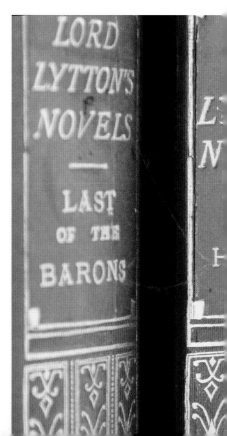

The resilience of paper

Archives are testament not only to the fact that printed matter occupies a large amount of present space, but that it has often previously occupied space in other places. Whether it is a single sheet folded to fit in a coat pocket, a stapled document on a desk or a personal collection of books occupying a whole room, printed paper is altered by those who have used it.

Although there are many natural hazards for printed paper, the worst damage is generally caused by human intervention. In earlier days, a new book was bought in loose-leaf form to be folded, sewn and bound by the owner to match an existing personal collection. But it was not uncommon for a previously owned book, perhaps a renowned 15th century book, to be stripped of its original cover and end sheets and replaced with covers to match the rest of the new owner's library. Today, to the chagrin of librarians and anyone who has ever bought books from a second-hand book shop, cash-strapped students have always ripped pages from books (art school students generally use a scalpel). Librarians are not entirely innocent either, sticking labels onto spines and rubber-stamping the title page and every colour plate inside in an attempt to deter their lenders from cutting them out. Students are also the prime suspects for highlighting, underlining and sophomoric marginal comments.

Natural signs of heavy wear caused by *normal* use: feathered page edges, creased corners and incidental marks, provide a book with a certain glow: signs of use suggest a useful or much-loved item. Hiroshi Ishii, aptly describes this phenomena. Having seen the original handwritten manuscript of Miyazawa Kenji's famous series of poems *The Last Farewell*, and lamented what had been lost in their transference to print, he returns to his own, personal 'dog-eared' paperback version: 'But there is one small consolation: there are traces of my own physical presence and of my

mind and spirit as a teenager in the paperback that travelled with me, in the many margin-jottings, stains and folded page corners scattered throughout it. That is why that beat-up old paperback is still there among my personal treasures.'[80]

A book's natural ageing process and 'the historic witness that it bears'[81] can only take place if the book was designed to have a long life. Signs of use – wear and tear – will undoubtedly be speeded up if the book is made with poor materials, which is why cheap paperbacks can so quickly become such personal and treasured items. The lightness and flexibility of paperbacks encourages them to be kept close to hand (Ishii carried *The Last Farewell* in his backpack when hostelling across Japan) whilst the eventual cracking of the binding and turned corners become permanent reminders of favourite pages. A casebound book, too heavy to carry long distances and designed with superior materials for a longer life, will tend to be handled with more care, nurtured, kept safe and dry in an allotted place.

The significance of a book's long-lived physical presence is demonstrated by the fact that book-sellers will, given the opportunity, provide the provenance of a book. This is possible because it was once common practice for the owner of a book to paste their personal book-plate onto the inside cover, and even today it is not unusual for an owner to write their name inside the book. In this way the ageing of a printed book, once one of an edition of many identical units, provides each with an identity all its own. When handling archived printed material, it is often the physical characteristics: size and weight, touch and smell,[82] together with its own very specific accumulated signs of use that can cause the researcher to re-examine received information about a document's age, purpose and function.

Young Romance through roses straying,
Unfold Truth trudge lamely on;
One in pleasures light was playing,
The other sighed for pleasures gone:
Cries Romance "Rest a minute
And discuss our views of earth:—
Yours may have most prudence in it,
But in mine is all the mirth."

Ah says Truth "this world discloses
Nought but vain delusive wiles,
Thorns are under all your roses,
Sadness follows all your smiles."
Cries Romance "Perhaps I soften
Colour life with tints too warm;
Yet my warmth a shade may soften,
While your coldness chills a charm."

"What is love?" the sage then asks him—
Love in summer hours so sweet?
Wintry weather soon unmasks him,
And your idol proves a cheat!"
Love "the youth replies, I sever
Real love from vain deceits;
Constant love brings hours that never
Lose their sunshine or their sweets"—

Friendship too, you call a treasure
But says Truth, it is a tie
Loosely woven mid scenes of pleasure,
And when Fortune frowns thrown by
"Friendship" he replies possesses
Worth which no dark change destroys,
Seeking, soothing our distresses
Sharing, doubling all our joys.

So says Truth, "tis plain we never
Can such hostile thoughts combine,
Folly is your guide for ever
While true sense must still be mine"
Cries the boy—"Frown on, no matter—
Mortals love my merry glance;
E'en in Truth's own path they scatter
Roses snatched from Young Romance

From the Cambridge Journal.—

On Procrastination   D. Y...

Be wise today; 'tis madness to defer;
Next day the fatal precedent will plead;
Thus on till wisdom is pushed out of Life.
Procrastination is the thief of time;
Year after year it steals till all are fled,
And to the mercies of a moment leaves
The vast concerns of an eternal scene.
Of Man's miraculous mistakes this bears
The palm, that all men are about to live,
For ever being on the brink of being born.
All pay themselves the compliment to think
They one day shall not drivel; and their fro...
On this reversion takes up ready prai...

Below:
Advertisement for Letraset 'instant lettering', 1964.

Below:
Cover, *Typographic*, 1982, (later *TypoGraphic*) journal of the International Society of Typographic Designers (ISTD) lamenting the damage inflicted on typographic standards by Letraset or, more accurately, its slapdash use by students.

Opposite page:
Letraset also produced bespoke sheets to order, enabling design consultancies to create accurate mock-ups and models for major clients. Later, multicolour sheets were also available.

Chapter 7:
Democratising graphic design

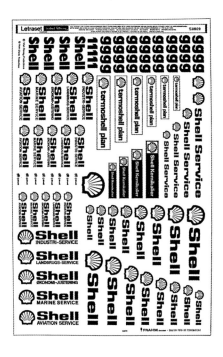

Before the desktop computer, graphic designers had few aids other than a tee-square, set-square and protractor with which to draw parallel, perpendicular or oblique lines. There was also a range of instruments for drawing circles, arcs and other curves (compasses, French curves, stencils, etc). It was a huge asset to be able to draw lettering by hand and some graphic designers specialised in this lucrative skill.

In the 1950s the Grant Projector was introduced and, despite its size and perfunctory appearance (see page 8) quickly became an essential piece of studio equipment because it enabled type specimens to be enlarged or reduced by projecting them upwards to a glass plate where a line-drawn copy could made onto tracing paper. It was, nevertheless, a slow task and the lamps made it uncomfortably hot work, so when Letraset, a new dry-transfer product, was introduced in London in 1959, its success was almost immediate.

Letraset
For the graphic designer, Letraset meant fewer hours working on a Grant Projector and fewer expensive visits to the typesetter. Any reasonably stocked studio would have a quantity of Letraset sheets stored in their boxes and housed in a Letraset-designed shelving system. At arm's length, a typeface would be available on several sheets each carrying a different point size. Initially, there were about thirty-five type-faces, including *Helvetica, Grot 9, Futura, Clarendon, Palace Script* and *Old English*. Type foundries considered Letraset to be a one-day wonder (Monotype's John Dreyfus called Letraset 'merely a toy')[83] but they would later regret agreeing so casually to generous licensing and copyright payments.

Letraset was able to respond quickly to the demand for new fashionable type-faces in the late 1960s and early 1970s because the process of bringing a font to production was relatively simple – certainly far simpler than that required by type foundries. The first of these was commissioned from Fred Lambert who designed *Compacta*, a bold condensed sans serif typeface which has proved to be timeless and yet sums up its own era so well. Using *Compacta*, a designer could take full advantage of Letraset's consummate manoeuvrability and seemed to encourage the designer to push the characters closer together – touching or even overlapping –

New Savings Plan

New Savings Plan

New Savings Plan

*New Savings Plan

something impossible to achieve with metal type. Because Letraset was used primarily for display rather than body text, its many iconic fonts, such as *Compacta* and Bob Newman's *Data 70* had a big influence on the appearance of print, capturing the optimism of the 60s and 70s. In all, 473 original faces were designed for Letraset, many of them initially released under the banner of the Letragraphica collection – available by subscription only.

The process of creating and making letterforms for Letraset would also have a significant long-term impact. Letraset characters were printed onto plastic sheets using a fine silk screen (serigraphic) printing process to provide crisp, opaque letterforms. This required stencil masters of the characters to be cut freehand from thin, deep-red Rubylith masking film.[84] Stencil-cutting was more than mere technique: trainees quickly learnt about letterform construction – stresses, proportions and curves – which had to be repeatedly cut until they had the perfect letter. This process proved a comprehensive grounding in all aspects of typeface design and some of the trainee stencil-cutters went on to become type designers in their own right, for example, Colin Brignall, Dave Farey, and Freda Sack, the last of which set up The Foundry with David Quay, another type designer who was commissioned by Letraset.

However, using Letraset was not without problems, and looking at printed material from that period one of the most common features is crooked alignment and uneven spacing of characters. This was, to some degree, due to the product itself. The plastic sheet on which the characters were printed tended to become distorted by the pressure applied when rubbing down a letter, but more significantly, it also demonstrated any shortfall in a designer's typographic knowledge or craft. Spacing marks were printed onto the sheets to help with intercharacter spacing and correct horizontal alignment, but these were often ignored. As a result, complaints about falling typographic standards became commonplace and, naturally, comparisons

Opposite page:
Letraset claimed to place the expertise of the graphic designer in the hands of everyone. Not only type but also rules, symbols, 'clip art' images, decorative borders and dummy text were available as Letraset products, c. 1964.

Below right:
Graphic Design Britain, 1967, edited and designed by Fred Lambert, using *Compacta*, the condensed sans serif typeface he designed for Letraset in 1963. Lambert taught typography at the London College of Printing, edited and designed the journal *Typos* and also organized several graphic design exhibitions and books to accompany them – *Graphic Design Britain*, is one of these.

were made with the outstanding quality achievable by Monotype and Linotype typesetting technologies. It was argued that the graphic designer had been served very well by the printer's compositor but had rarely appreciated the knowledge and skills that went into the service received.

During the period that Letraset was at its most influential, a new typesetting technology was evolving that purported to offer typesetting comparable in quality to metal but with the flexibility and inclusivity of Letraset.

Phototypesetting

By the 1960s most commercial work was being printed by lithography but all typography – certainly textual material, and often headlines, rules etc – was still produced using metal type via Monotype, Linotype or other similar typesetting machines. A printed proof would be cut and pasted-up to form the artwork before being transferred to lithographic plates via photographic process.

Phototypesetting effectively eliminated metal type. What is more, phototypesetting, it was argued, could be available within the confines of the designer's own studio to make the creative process more flexible and less time-constrained. In reality, the technology proved too complex (each manufacturer implemented their own unique coding scheme) too expensive and its maintenance too daunting a prospect for most design studios to consider buying. Instead, phototypesetting machines were bought by larger-scale publisher/printers whilst a bold new breed of specialist independent typesetting companies were established to serve a growing graphic design community.

Phototypesetting proved to be the death knell of the commercial letterpress printer and during the 1970s printing companies began disposing of their letterpress

Above:
The Harris-Intertype Fototronic disc, developed in the late 1960s. A disc might hold a font in roman, italic and, perhaps two weights. As the disc spun at high speed a light would flash at the appropriate moment through the negative letter on the disc to expose and 'transfer' the letter in place on to light-sensitive photographic paper.

Above right:
Cover of a promotional booklet, 1950, for the Fotosetter, a photographic line composing machine manufactured by Intertype. This early but technically complex phototypesetting technology retains some of the characteristics of the previous Monotype and Linotype hot metal casters.

typesetting equipment, proofing and printing presses, and often hundreds of cases of type accumulated over the previous half century. Those printers who were able, transferred their efforts to lithography. Not surprisingly, phototypesetting was equally devastating for traditional type foundries. The German type foundry Berthold invested heavily in developing its own phototypesetting systems and, indeed, led the European higher-quality typesetting market for a period. But for many traditional type foundries, closure or even bankruptcy was inevitable and with it went generations of unique knowledge and craftsmanship which, so it was argued, was now irrelevant.

Early phototypesetting machines from manufacturers such as Compugraphic, Mergenthaler/Linotype, Alphatype, Intertype, Photon, Lumitype and Autologic, had little or no text storage capability and display screens offered only a vague approximation of what, exactly, the final outcome would look like. The typesetting operator worked with marked-up copy from the designer. Output was limited to the width of the photographic paper, which came as a roll, and so required the type-setting to be manoeuvred to fit as economically as possible. Once delivered to the designer, these 'galley proofs' (a term left over from letterpress technology) were cut

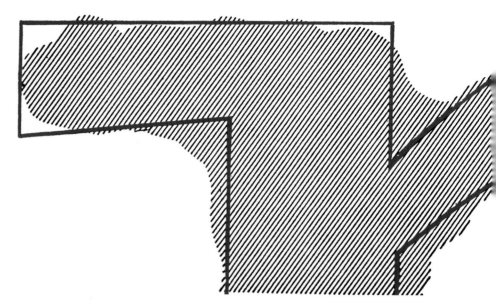

pp
—
pp

Above:
An illustration of the distortive effect of light exposure on letterforms and how adjustments in design can minimise distortion. This represents printed 7pt type enlarged.

Below:
Matthew Carter, *Bell Centennial*, designed in 1978 for exclusive use in AT&T's telephone directories. To negate the effect of light-spread in the photo-typsetting process, as well the effects of ink spread during printing, additional spaces (called 'ink-traps') were created. Printed in the smaller point sizes used in telephone directories, the ink-traps are not visible, having done their job by filling in and smoothing out the character stroke (see page 142).

Opposite page, top:
E13B and the grid in which it is constructed.

and pasted into position on the final artwork. The smell of the waxing machine (used to provide a thin coat of warm molten wax to the back of each individual cut-out bit of text to act as an adhesive) pervaded design studios well into the 1980s.

The photographic nature of phototypesetting – essentially, flashing a light through a moving negative film or spinning disc to expose each letterform onto light-sensitive paper – meant that the corners of letterforms appeared soft or rounded and so type-faces were adjusted to reduce this effect. Adrian Frutiger, who was commissioned to redraw fonts for Lumitype phototypesetting, complained that, 'The fonts [I redrew] don't have any historical worth...to think of the sort of aberrations I had to produce in order to see a good result on Lumitype! V and W needed huge crotches in order to stay open. I nearly had to introduce serifs in order to prevent rounded-off corners – instead of a sans serif the drafts were a bunch of misshapen sausages!'[85]

Phototypesetting was a miserable development for the typographer and for type design generally. However, one consequence was that typesetting programs designed to drive phototypesetting machines helped pave the way towards the development of Desk Top Publishing (DTP) software programs.

NOPQRSTUVW

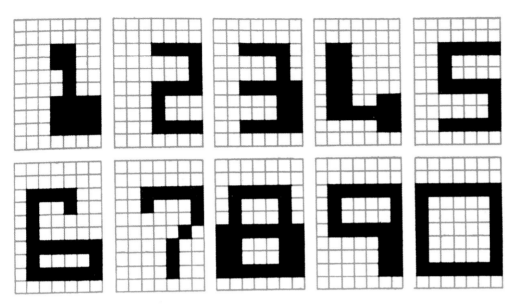

Adapting letterforms for technologies

Magnetic Ink Character Recognition code is a character-recognition technology developed during the 1950s to be used by the banking industry to automate the processing of cheques and similar documents. The technology allows a machine to 'read' (scan and record) information, but it was also essential that MICR characters could be read by humans, and so a barcode or similar device was unsuitable. Stanford Research Institute and General Electric Computer Laboratory developed the first automated system using MICR and the same engineering team developed the *E13B,* MICR font. By the end of 1959, the first cheques had been printed using *E13B.* (*E* refers to the font being the fifth considered, and *B* to the fact that it was the second version. The *13* refers to the 0.013 inch character grid.)

E13B proved to be remarkably 'legible', remaining recognisable (by machine and human) even through finger marks or over-stamping. It is still used today for auto-mating tasks such as passport processing, postal tracking, consumer goods packaging (batch codes, lot codes, expiration dates), and clinical applications as well as for cheques and other financial documents. But probably to the surprise of its makers, the distinctive appearance of *E13B,* and its association with new technology, caught the imagination of designers.

Leo Maggs, in 1964 was working in Covent Garden, London when he was asked 'to draw, in a "futuristic" style', a title for a magazine article. 'Only a few words were needed and I opted to draw them in caps based on *E13B,* used on bank cheques. Having completed the task to everyone's satisfaction I decided to complete the alphabet in my spare time.' Once completed, albeit still only including caps and figures, Maggs submitted his design to Letraset who rejected it as 'commercially unviable'. Maggs then approached one of London's first phototypesetting companies, Photoscript Ltd, who added the font to their catalogue and called it *Westminster,*

Below:
OCR–A (Optical Character Recognition) produced by the American Type Foundry (ATF) in 1968 to be 'read' by machines.

Opposite page, top:
Traditional textual letter reproduced using a grid corresponding to a TV monitor resolution and Wim Crouwel's alternative. Crouwel designed *New Alphabet* to be capable of being translated exactly as intended, without distortion.

Opposite page, bottom:
Wim Crouwel's *New Alphabet* was popular enough to be generated by Letter Press, the Dutch subsidiary of Mecanorma, Letraset's main rival, c. late 1960s.

(perhaps after the National Westminster Bank, as it was then known, in acknowledgement of the font's origins in the banking industry).[86] It proved remarkably popular and several similar fonts quickly appeared including *Countdown*, designed by Colin Brignall, 1965 and *Data 70*, designed by Bob Newman, 1970 – both commissioned by Letraset.

In 1968, American Type Founders produced *OCR–A*, one of the first optical character recognition typefaces to meet criteria set by the US Bureau of Standards. Although OCR technology has since advanced to the point where such fonts are no longer necessary, the monoline *OCR–A* font with its highly distinct forms and mechanical inter-character spacing is occasionally used when 'futuristic' technologies requires expression.

The adaptation of letterforms for early digital technologies began with the cathode ray tube (CRT) monitor, developed first for television and used in the development of phototypesetting in the mid-1960s, in which digitally stored information was reconfigured to represent characters on-screen for the first time. The form of the character was stored as a crude bitmapped image comprised of individual pixels.[87]

The jagged visual effect of a severely limited number of pixels being available to describe something as complex as Roman letterforms was the impetus for a number of designers to consider the design of a unique font that could function on CRT screens effectively despite the technical restraints. This caused a reappraisal of those typefaces associated with the Bauhaus during the 1920s that had been constructed of the 'fundamental grammar of visual communication': the square, circle and triangle.[88] One of the most important and striking of these was *New Alphabet*, a parametric typeface designed by Wim Crouwel and released in 1967.

New Alphabet began as a personal experimental project of Wim Crouwel. The typeface was designed to embrace the limitations of the cathode ray tube technology

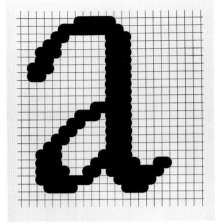

used by early data display screens and phototypesetting equipment, and thus chiefly uses horizontal and vertical strokes. Crouwel wanted to adapt his design to work for the new technologies, instead of adapting the technologies to meet the design: 'The machine has to be accepted as essential if we are to cope with the demands of our age. The quantity of information which must, of necessity be printed daily has increased to such an extent that mechanization is indispensable. The inconsistency now becomes more apparent. The letters have never evolved with the machines.' [89] His proposed unconventional alphabet was intended merely as an initial step in a direction which could possibly be followed by research with cathode ray technology as the starting point for its means of reproduction.

Most of the letters are based on a grid of five by nine units, with forty-five degree corners. There is no differentiation between upper-case and lower-case letterforms. Many of his peers were of the opinion that the design was too unconventional, but

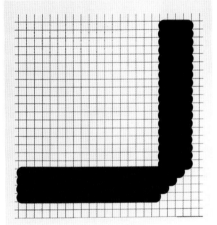

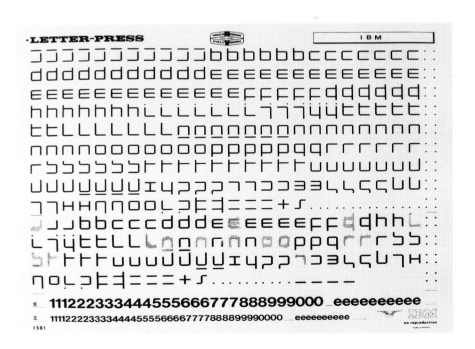

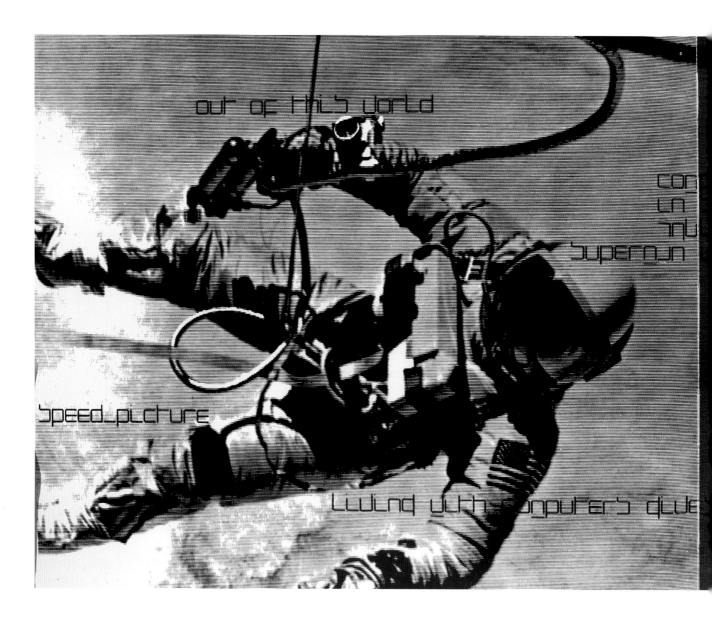

Above:
A page from *New Alphabet*, 1967, a sixteen-page booklet about Wim Crouwel's typeface, one of a series of booklets designed to promote the typographic company De Jong & Co.

Opposite page:
Jan Tschichold, design for a single alphabet typeface, Germany, 1929. One of several Bauhaus-inspired 'elemental' typefaces based upon the 'fundamental grammar of communication' that were reappraised during the 1970s.

the typeface received a lot of newspaper coverage and created a lively debate concerning typefaces as art compared to the pressing practicalities involved in their purpose.[90] Dependency on basic forms and emphasis on horizontal and vertical lines inevitably encouraged comparisons between Crouwel's *New Alphabet* and the typefaces associated with the Bauhaus and De Stijl during the 1920s. But whilst for artists and designers such as Theo van Doesburg, Herbert Bayer, Jan Tschichold, Bart van der Leck and Max Bill, the process was driven by ideology, *New Alphabet* was designed to solve a specific practical problem.

für den neuen m
nur das gleichg

Typography and the computer

For most designers the digital age began January 1984 with the launch of the Apple Macintosh personal computer. The concept of 'Desk Top Publishing' was effectively launched the following year by the Aldus Corporation and its software program PageMaker in co-operation with Apple. This alliance, together with the Apple LaserWriter, the first 'desktop' printer compatible with PostScript (enabling the printer to match what is on the computer screen) and, later, Adobe Illustrator, 1987, and Adobe Photoshop, 1990, made it possible for the graphic designer to achieve commercial typographic work for the first time without recourse to outside services before delivering artwork to the printer. Everything, from an office memo or village newsletter to the design of a commercially printed magazine or 496-page book was now possible for *anyone* to achieve with a 'Mac'.

It had been a long time coming and its consequences and commercial and creative potential had been discussed for decades. Yet, when the first desktop computer arrived it still felt sudden and shocking – the adoption of terminology from previous typographic technologies is testament to this. Even the term 'foundry' was (and is still today) used to describe the studio of a type designer, despite the process being entirely digital. One of the earliest and most influential of these new 'foundries' was the Adobe Originals program in San Jose, California.

Founded in 1983, Adobe Systems Incorporated, the renowned computer software company, also began to educate itself regarding typography and, in 1989, set up the Adobe Originals type design program by hiring Carol Twombly and Robert Slimbach to work as in-house type designers. Ambitious intentions were demonstrated by the extent to which Adobe took on the cultural role that better typeface manufacturing companies had done in their heyday. The first two new typefaces were Slimbach's *Utopia* and *Adobe Garamond*. Adobe already had contracts to digitise and sell fonts by companies such as the International Typeface Corporation but felt that many of these had a somewhat dated appearance. Adobe's printed promotional material, published to accompany the launch of each new typeface, included a comprehensive display of the typeface supported by informative essays and bibliographies, together

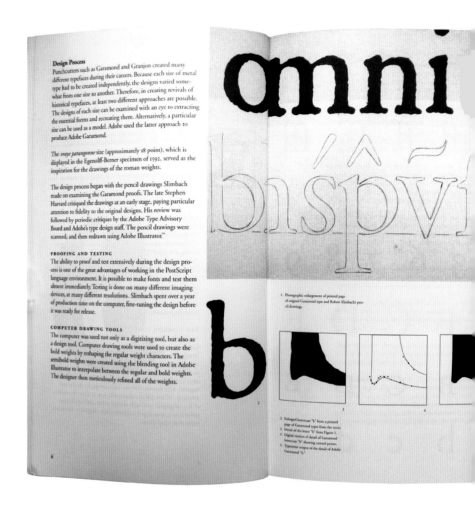

Design Process
Punchcutters such as Garamond and Granjon created many different typefaces during their careers. Because each size of metal type had to be created independently, the designs varied somewhat from one size to another. Therefore, in creating revivals of historical typefaces, at least two different approaches are possible. The designs of each size can be examined with an eye to extracting the essential forms and recreating them. Alternatively, a particular size can be used as a model. Adobe used the latter approach to produce Adobe Garamond.

The *moye parangonne* size (approximately 18 point), which is displayed in the Egenolff-Berner specimen of 1592, served as the inspiration for the drawings of the roman weights.

The design process began with the pencil drawings Slimbach made on examining the Garamond proofs. The late Stephen Harvard critiqued the drawings at an early stage, paying particular attention to fidelity to the original designs. His review was followed by periodic critiques by the Adobe Type Advisory Board and Adobe's type design staff. The pencil drawings were scanned, and then redrawn using Adobe Illustrator.'"

PROOFING AND TESTING
The ability to proof and test extensively during the design process is one of the great advantages of working in the PostScript language environment. It is possible to make fonts and test them almost immediately. Testing is done on many different imaging devices, at many different resolutions. Slimbach spent over a year of production time on the computer, fine-tuning the design before it was ready for release.

COMPUTER DRAWING TOOLS
The computer was used not only as a digitizing tool, but also as a design tool. Computer drawing tools were used to create the bold weights by reshaping the regular weight characters. The semibold weights were created using the blending tool in Adobe Illustrator to interpolate between the regular and bold weights. The designer then meticulously refined all of the weights.

1. Photographic enlargement of printed page of original Garamond type and Robert Slimbach's pencil drawings.

2. Enlarged lowercase 'b' from a printed page of Garamond type from the 1500s.
3. Detail of the letter 'b' from Figure 1.
4. Digital version of detail of Garamond lowercase 'b' showing control points.
5. Typesetter output of the detail of Adobe Garamond 'b'.

6

Emperor 8

Emperor 10

Emperor 15

Emperor 19

with specimens of the type carefully designed in action. These early fonts were influenced by research into the calligraphy and classic types from the 15th and 16th centuries. Just how far digital software had developed can be judged by comparing Adobe Original fonts with those created by Zuzana Licko just ten years earlier using a first-generation Macintosh computer.

Whilst Adobe was making the technological headlines, Bitstream Inc, can claim to be the first digital foundry. Although located in Massachusetts, its founding partners, Matthew Carter and Mike Parker, were originally from England and drew on their understanding and appreciation of European typography without losing sight of the particular requirements of digital technology. For example, Carter's typeface *Charter*, designed in 1987, might well have its origins in the French type cutter and founder Pierre-Simon Fournier's 18th century characters, but it was designed to overcome the digital problem of limited memory. Carter later explained:

There was an issue about the amount of data required to store fonts. A serif typeface took twice as much data as a sans, because of all the curves and extra points. So I started doing *Charter* with a very simplified structure and a minimum

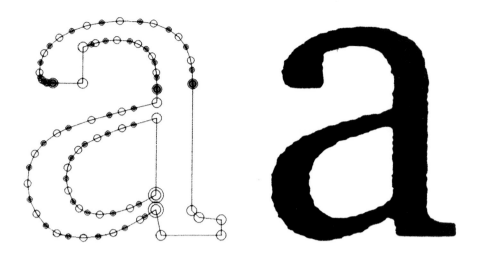

Opposite page, top:
Spread from Adobe Originals' type specimen and promotional booklet for Robert Slimbach's *Adobe Garamond* that provided information regarding the origins of the typeface and its digital development. California, 1983.

Opposite page, bottom:
Zuzana Licko, *Emperor*, designed using the newly released type design program, Fontographer in 1984. Licko's wholehearted commitment to digital technology was demonstrated by the creation a typeface range that celebrated its technical 'limitations'.

Above:
Matthew Carter, *Charter*, designed for Bitstream Inc, 1987. The design of *Charter* was optimised for use with low-memory computers and for printing on low-resolution laser printers by limiting the use of curves in favour of straight-line segments. *Charter* lowercase 'a'; outline showing the digitised points; the same typeset at 1,000 lines/inch and printed at 14pt on a laser printer image.

number of curves, more straight-line segments, etc. [...] When finished, I proudly went to the head of engineering at Bitstream, but he said: oh, we don't have a problem with that any longer, we now have more compact algorithms. I was left with a design solution to a nonexistent technical problem. But by that time I had gotten very interested in the idea of the simplified design. The technical *raison d'etre* had gone, but I persevered with it for completely different reasons, as I was now interested in the design for its own sake.[91]

Matthew Carter left to set up his own independent 'foundry' whilst Bitstream's font business was acquired by Monotype Imaging in 2012. Monotype is one of several celebrated older companies established in 19th century foundry type making and typesetting machinery – others include Linotype, now Linotype-Hell, and Berthold AG, now Berthold Types Ltd. All have survived in one form or another via difficult forced marriages and remarriages, adoptions and readoptions, by transnational controlling corporations.

Touchscreen handwriting recognition

While Apple's Newton proved to be a financial disappointment for the company, this was their first touchscreen device and, weighing just one pound (0.45 kilogram) it also paved the way for future innovations in mobile technology. The Newton was marketed as a personal digital assistant (PDA) but it was the pen-based touchscreen interface that gave the MessagePad its distinctive character. Lacking a keyboard, the Newton depended on handwriting recognition for text-based user input, a 'futuristic' feature that caught the public's imagination. Called *Calligrapher*, the original hand-writing recognition system attempted to learn the user's natural handwriting, using a database of known words to calculate what the user was writing. It could also interpret writing anywhere on the screen. Unfortunately, the writing recognition system in this first version was notoriously bad, and though it subsequently improved, the Newton never recovered. By contrast, the PalmPilot, a rival touch-screen PDA launched in 1996, had a far simpler, single-stroke 'shorthand' hand-writing recognition system, called *Graffiti*: a preordained alphabet the user had to learn and use.

Designed by Jeff Hawkins, *Graffiti* used letter shapes which resembled standard handwritten letterforms modified to provide added differentiation. Other touch-screen systems used traditional left-to-right writing, the drawback being that users quickly ran out of screen space. With *Graffiti*, the user wrote one letter on top of another, lifting the pen between each. This meant that every letter had to be described in one continuous stroke (for example, it would be impossible to dot an 'i'). The single stroke concept was necessary for the computer to recognize each individual letter and the order in which they were written. *Graffiti* was based primarily on upper-case characters but because each had to be written with a single stroke, four of the characters, A, F, K and T required modification.

PalmPilot was a success and encouraged a long line of stylus-based personal digital assistants from Palm, HP, Dell and others. When Apple returned to touch-screen technology with the iPhone in 2007, it was clear that they had paid close attention to developments since the disappointment of Newton. Crucially, the iPhone enabled the user to engage in a number of interconnected communication activities – browse the Web, make calls, notes and handle e-mail – all rather well.

Supplementary Sheets

ROBERT BESLEY & Cº LONDON.

Below:
Newspapers have been transformed by digital media in the last thirty years. First, new technology broke the traditional working methods, vigorously defended by the print unions, and enabled the graphic designer to play a more significant role. Second, newspapers are no longer the prime source of 'breaking news' and so their role has become one of analysis and comment, allowing general interest topics to dominate newspaper 'tops'.

Felicity Cloake's
perfect apricot tart

£2.00 (Ch. Islands £2.40
Thursday 08.09.16
Published in London
and Manchester
theguardian.com

th

Loadsamoney

3 The rehabilitation of print and printed media

Below:
Newspaper journalists working on word processors at
the *Wolverhampton Express and Star*, c. early 1980s.
Previously, copy had been generated on typewriters
which then had to be 'keyboarded' again by type-
setters using Monotype or, more commonly in the
newspaper industry, Linotype machines, from which
the copy was then cast as metal type.
  Now called the *Express and Star*, this local newspaper has established a strong digital presence
whilst maintaining its printed version.

Opposite page:
The physical presence of international newspapers
on display on city streets, airport terminals and rail
stations remains an important source of publicity for
publishers, despite the growing popularity of their
online digital versions.

Chapter 8:
Print media adapting to digital tools

The nature of the Internet favours transitory information, which is why newspapers have been so vulnerable to its development, a situation not helped by the newspaper industry taking so long to recognise the threat of digital technology. The future viability of the newspaper is an on-going news story.

Newspapers: Managing transition

Most major newspapers now have a strong and authoritative digital presence although their transference remains in flux. *The New York Times* is a case in point. The paper has had a Web presence since 1996. Initially, some articles were freely available but others required registration. In 2005, the paper introduced a subscription-based service, called TimesSelect, whilst remaining free for print copy subscribers. This was discontinued two years later, and, for about three years nytimes.com was a free site. In 2011, a metered subscription was reintroduced, allowing 'occasional' readers (up to ten visits per month) free access, but on the eleventh visit the reader was asked to pay the full subscription. This model, with variations for different platforms, reflects the current (2016) situation, but across the spectrum of newspapers there remain huge variations as each tries to find the magic formula.

The credibility provided by the long-standing omnipresence and strong brand recognition of surviving dailies has been hugely beneficial whilst newspaper publishers attempt to realign their businesses and learnt how best to utilise new media. It was initially thought that the volume of written material needed to be reduced for reading on screens – although it is also probable that this was done as an incentive to readers to continue buying the newspaper which carried the full version. However today, with relatively simple, though important typographic adjustments (choice of typeface, tracking, adjustment to the tone of black etc.) articles that appear in the printed newspaper are generally also displayed in full on screen. In fact, since there are no space restrictions there is every opportunity to provide additional information on screen. Links to 'related content' or to previously published reports on a particular topic – as well as hyperlinks to source material – demonstrates how much the newspaper industry has, eventually, begun to embrace the potential of digital technology.

Below right:
Heading blocks designed by Raymond Hawkey
for the *Daily Express* during the 1960s, incorporating
stylistic developments in television and film-based
media.

Bottom:
Diagram stretching the width of two newspaper
pages, designed by Malcom Topp and drawn by
Roy Castle for the *Daily Express*, 1965.

Whilst their online sophistication develops, the sales of the traditional
newspapers continue to fall. The rate of fall has fluctuated, but across the industry
averages of seven percent each year are not unusual. A small number of papers have
bucked this trend, but many others have suffered far larger, sometimes catastrophic
falls. For example, in San Francisco, a particularly new media-conscious city, *The
San Francisco Chronicle* lost almost twenty-three per cent of its weekday sales during
recession-hit 2009.[92]

One of the effects of digital transference has been a distinct and concentrated
effort to improve the overall design of their paper versions. The long-term strategy
of investing additional effort and funds into paper and ink – an aspect of the business
that appears to be on the wane – reflects the high status that print retains for these
companies. Their display outside news vendors and transport hubs, as well as the

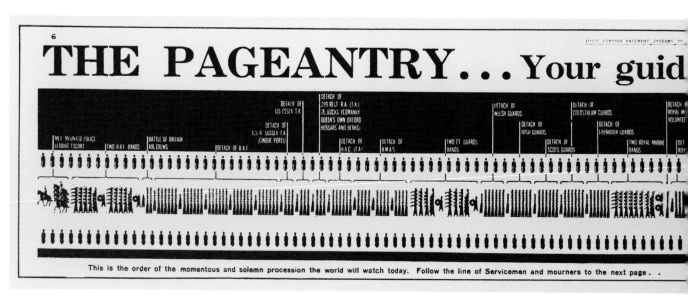

sight of travellers immersed in their newspaper is a constant reminder of their presence. (There may be an equal number reading their 'paper' online, but who would know?) More fundamental, revenue from advertising in print, though dwindling, remained more lucrative than advertising raised for inclusion on their online sites. This trend was, finally, reversed in 2016.

The industry's reluctance to embrace the idea of accessing their newspapers on screen is not surprising. Between 1900 and 1960 little had fundamentally changed in the compositing and printing of newspapers – a branch of the printing industry particularly averse to change – instead, it had been more about refining, consolidating and increasing output in order to more efficiently meet demand. However, an appreciation of what the designer might contribute was of growing interest in the 1960s, due in large part to the popular influence of innovate design seen in television and magazines. It was at this time that many newspapers began including additional sections and 'weekend' magazine supplements.

But it was the move from metal to digital technology in the 1980s that caused the revolution in working methods and practices within newspaper production. In the hands of the traditionally trained print compositor, letterpress composition and printing had meant that the layout of newspapers was a formulaic process. However, digital technology introduced a new flexibility that enabled all aspects of newspaper work to be fully integrated: writing; photography; editing; picture editing; designing and printing. The flexibility of digital technology was at odds with the methods and skills of the letterpress compositors and printers, indeed, the introduction of digital technology into the newspaper industry was resisted with all the strength the print unions could muster. But once broken the previous hierarchy was swiftly dismantled and one of the earliest beneficiaries was the designer who quickly began to have greater more influence on the appearance and functionality of newspapers. 'Layout' was no longer a technical process, it could now be a creative one.

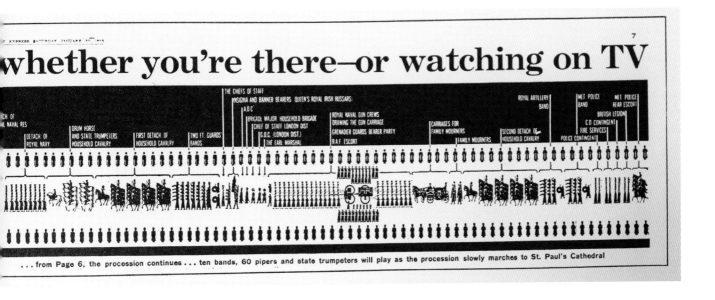

. . . from Page 6, the procession continues . . . ten bands, 60 pipers and state trumpeters will play as the procession slowly marches to St. Paul's Cathedral

Competition, between newspapers and with other media, was the driving force behind print innovation, and the introduction of computers in editorial offices was the starting point of the design revolution. Even in the 1970s and early 80s, readers often already knew about the main news events from television or the radio and so newspaper editors sought to provide something extra. Many more words, in the form of analysis and comment, was one of the solutions. The single, compact newspaper gave way to one that was divided up into loose thematic supplements, first at weekends, then alternate days of the week, the aim being to provide a broader and more in-depth reading experience.

During the 1990s, and coinciding with the growing presence of the Internet, newspapers began to place more emphasis on presenting a cohesive, interconnected presentation for the various news stories it contains. Photography, graphic design and typography were given more prominent roles. Indeed, their overt presence was initially irksome to many regular readers who considered all this to be no more than superficial frippery and an impairment to the free and unfettered communication of information.

It is true that having been given the task of making the newspaper compete, not only with rival newspapers and magazines but also the Internet, the hand of the graphic designer had become particularly conspicuous. Since the majority of a newspaper's audience were (and remain) regular daily readers it was quickly realised that this tactic was counterproductive and a degree of calm was reintroduced.

A significant aspect of the new approach to overall design was that the number of articles on a page was dramatically reduced. More remarkable still was that areas of space were built into the page structure to allow breathing space within and between articles. The adherence to a new reader-led (as apposed to production-led) approach – introduced by the graphic designer – is best demonstrated by the way short items, which had previously been used as 'fillers' to plug gaps literally anywhere in the paper, were now more often collected together and printed as a single column.

Whilst the nature of the Internet has had an influence on the design of newspapers, the development of newspaper websites has, of necessity, had to find a very different way of functioning from the print version. Here, there is generally no longer a front 'page' with an eye-catching headline, large photograph and leading article. Instead, the reader is presented with what is, effectively, a contents page: a list of articles grouped under headings such as 'Headlines', 'Highlights', 'Sport', 'Opinion', 'People' etc, all using the same size and style of typeface, some supported with a small photograph. Once accessed, an article is presented as a single column of text, intersected by advertisements. This digital 'top-down' pyramid structure means that it is almost certain that the whole 'paper' will never be seen, let alone read. Marissa Mayer, Google's vice-president of 'search products and user experience', explained to a US Senate hearing on The Future of Journalism (2009): 'The structure of the Web has caused the [...] consumption of news to migrate from the full newspaper to the individual article. As with music and video, many people still consume physical newspapers in their original full-length format. But with online news, a reader is much more likely to arrive at a single article. While these

Above:
Berthold Kohler (second left) one of the publishers of Germany's national newspaper *Frankfurter Allgemeine Zeitung* (FAZ), Christian Pohlert (fifth left) leader of the newspaper's picture department and other photo and text editors gather to discuss the choice of cover headline and photographs for 4 October 2007. The flexibility of digital technology enables a more inclusive design and editorial process. (Compare with the photograph on page 8.)

This was the last edition of the newspaper to feature its traditional Gothic masthead.

individual articles can be accessed from a newspaper's home page, readers often click directly to a particular article via a search engine or another web site.' [93]

The result is that authority is taken away from the newspaper's editor (together with the executive editors and specialist subject assistant editors and designer) and placed in the hands of the user. Editors are generally far from self-effacing individuals, but in the overall scheme of things their contribution goes largely unnoticed by the reader. However, their efforts in directing the focus and organisation of information across a newspaper is valuable and one that contributes considerably to the page-by-page reading experience. This expertise is closely aligned to the editorial design of each page, spread and section, with considered placement of headlines, photographs, infographics, quotes etc, which together, provide a rich and informative reading experience. The on-screen single-column equivalent, and lacking any sense of being a coherent whole, is vastly diminished in comparison.

Below:

The Face, magazine designed by Neville Brody offering an exhuberant and idiosyncratic reading experience reminicent of the 'cut and paste' fanzine, although, as Brody later explained, 'design was the [real] content'. This issue is from 1983.

Below right:

Industria, a typeface designed by Neville Brody c.1984 for headline use in *The Face. Industria* was commercially released as a font in 1989/90.

From fanzine to mainstream

In magazine publishing, as with newspapers, the arrival of digital technology meant that the designer was given a great deal more autonomy. But whilst the unpredictable nature of a newspaper's content required design to provide clarity and restraint, a magazine that focused on a specific subject area could have a distinctive voice and appearance all its own. In effect, the more specialist the subject the smaller the editorial group and the greater the amount of freedom afforded to the designer.

This is reminiscent of the vigorously independent character of the fanzines whose most influential period was coming to an end as digital technology began to take hold. Indeed, although some aspects of the design of this new generation of 'mainstream' commercial magazines was, of necessity, achieved via computer screens, a significant part of their design was still created by hand-cutting and pasting down words, marks and photographs onto art board, photocopying and using a photocopy machine to help manipulate type and images – before being transferred by various means to the computer. The obvious difference, however, between the new digital, commercially printed and bound magazines, and their fanzine counterparts, was in production values. Magazines such as Neville Brody's *The Face* (1981–1986) and

Below:
A double-page spread from *Issues*, (number 8) the journal of the Design Museum, designed by Cartlidge Levene, London who looked to the sharp refinement of mainland Europe for inspiration, in particular the work of Wolfgang Weingart and Wim Crouwel. Printed silver and black, 1992.

Terry Jones' *i–D*, (which began as a hand-stapled fanzine in 1980) both UK, were highly idiosyncratic, to the point that the content was, effectively, their design.

Running alongside these magazines was the influential typography magazine *Emigre*. This was published between 1984 and 2005 in Berkeley, California, and designed and edited by Dutch-born Rudy VanderLans using fonts designed by his wife, Czechoslovakian-born Zuzana Licko. It was, in essence, a fanzine for typographers. Together, VanderLans and Licko's use and committed embrace of this new technology was a revelation for those graphic designers who had had misgivings about the move to desk top publishing. *Emigre* made the computer desirable by demonstrating its flexibility as a creative tool, and as the technology became increasingly responsive – in VanderLans hands even amorphic – so too did the appearance of *Emigre*. Headings overlapped, columns of text swerved across the page and photographs as the necessity of a grid dissolved. This was a striking development because the universal 20th century graphic vocabulary had remained stubbornly modernist, largely because it had the 'virtue' of providing predictability – to the point of being neutral – in an increasingly multi-international and multi-lingual corporate culture. But VanderLans rejected this overtly structured approach

Above and opposite page, top left:

Emigre #22, 1992, cover and spread. Editor and
designer Rudy VandeLans invited contributions from
many designers and this issue includes a 'typeface'
by Nick Bell called *Psycho,* which took the form of
random 'stab wounds'. The folded brown paper insert
was handprinted and 'wounded' by Bell assisted by
students at the London College of Printing, a process
recorded in the two small photographs at the bottom
of the page. The cover's photographic collage was
designed by Andy Rumball.

in favour of a relaxation of grid strictures that allowed a refreshing unpredictability.
Emigre was provocative, in both its writing and appearance and VanderLans and
Licko's unreserved commitment to digital technology – until then suspected by many
designers to be devoid, or even restrictive of creative potential – helped morph the
computer, and the Mac in particular, into an essential tool required by every design
studio with innovative ambition.

Emigre's large format (285 mm x 425 mm until 1995) was, of itself, unconventional
– closer to a broadsheet newspaper than a magazine. VanderLans described it as 'a
magazine that ignores boundaries'. Its generous page size provided large, dramatic
fields of ink and contrasting white spaces with dense, distinctively shaped, jaggedly
textured areas of text. Although usually limited to a single colour it was never

Above right:

Emigre, full page advertisement for Barry Deck's 'unforgivable' typeface *Template Gothic*, 'type that reflects the imperfect language of an imperfect world', distributed by *Emigre*. Deck, celebrating *Emigre's* lack of historical prescience, included quizzical critics comments and finishes by saying 'I'm not asking for forgiveness, but please buy my font'.

lacking in visual bravura, and a series of guest designers helped ensure it rarely failed to surprise (for example, see page 57). The fact that *Emigre* – a magazine about type – could be found alongside music magazines such as *The Face* and, later, *Ray Gun* in record stores provided additional kudos. The choice of an uncoated paper gave the ink – often dark blue or green – a distinct, dense sheen.

The rise of digital technology meant that even before 1990 the necessity of *printing* a magazine was being questioned. Disk magazines (or 'diskmags') were magazines stored on a disk contained in a printed jacket to be read on a computer or printed out using a desk-top printer. The rise of the Internet caused their demise, but the inclusion of a disk, usually attached to a magazine cover and carrying 'bonus' digital material, continued to be used, especially by computer magazines. However, in 1991, when Neville Brody and Jon Wozencroft set about editing and designing *Fuse*, the disk itself became, once more, the focus of the 'magazine' content. Published quarterly by FontShop, its outward presence was a sturdy cardboard box that held the disk which contained four new and experimental fonts. In addition, there was an editorial sheet with texts by Wozencroft or guest authors and four folded posters, each acting as a 'specimen sheet' showcasing a typeface. Themes set by the editors, such as 'Codes', 'Crash', 'Religion', would be playfully subverted by the invited contributors. The box was an ideal foil for the free-form, often structureless nature of the material it contained.

The fonts in *Fuse* demonstrated new levels of digital fluency by their designers. The designer could now clearly dominate the technology to the point (like the pencil or paint brush before) of making the means by which the font was made dissolve from view. But as Brody explained in an interview in 1992, the designer had to remain vigilant: 'If you are going to use a computer you have to really struggle with it, otherwise it will make all the decisions for you. The default mechanism means that if you don't specify the angle of a line, it will draw a straight vertical line. If you don't select a typeface, it will select one for you. I see so many Macintosh gimmicks [or default 'solutions'] in a designer's work.'[94] Indeed, three years later at the *Fuse* conference in Berlin, Jon Wozencroft warned typographers not to 'collapse into the digital maelstrom', but rather, 'reach for the language of sensuality'[95] and maintain contact with the raw materials and tools away from

Above:
The Designers Republic™, this play on the famous Paul Rand logo design for Westinghouse (page 50) was positioned prominently on the first page of their design of *Emigre* magazine number 29 (page 56) and followed irreverently by a line referencing the Sex Pistols album (page 67) 'Never mind Paul Rand, here's The Designers Republic'. 1994.

Above right:
Robert Nakata, Diligentia Seizoen logo designed in collaboration with Studio Dunbar, Holland, 1988. An identity for a season of musical events. The Dunbar studio established a distinct break from the increasingly predictable geometric corporate logo solutions of the previous generation of Dutch design companies such as Total Design.

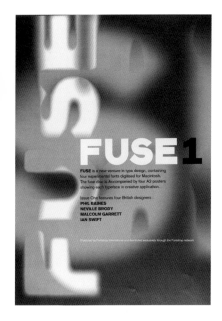

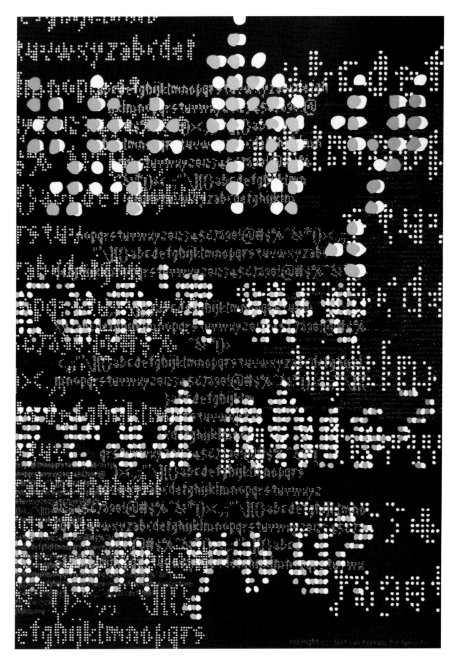

Above:
Neville Brody, poster for *Fuse*, a quarterly 'magazine',
1991. Edited by Brody and Jon Wozencroft and
published initially by FontShop. The magazine took
the form of a cardboard box containing a compact
disc with four experimental fonts digitised for the
MacIntosh computer, and four A2 posters 'showing
each typeface in creative application'.

Above right:
Poster for *Flixel*, designed by Just van Rossum for
Fuse, inspired by LED displays, 1992.

Right:
Barry Deck's typeface, *Caustic Biomorph*, 1992.

ABCDEFGHIJKLMN
OPQRSTUVWXYZ?!:;
1234567890

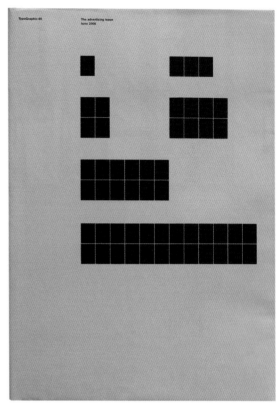

Above:
Shops exclusively selling magazines, such as this one in Amsterdam, have appeared following the explosion in independent publishing.

Above right:
The flexibility of digital technology encouraged a new enthusiasm for magazines edited, published and designed by graphic designers. *TypoGraphic* is the journal of the International Society of Typographic Designers (ISTD). Editor David Jury (1996–2006) commissioned a different designer for each issue chosen for their sympathy to the given theme. This issue, concerning typography and advertising, was co-designed by Paul Belford (working as an independent Art Director and renowned for his inventive use of typography) and David Jury. The 'face' is made utilising standard UK billboard poster formats.

the computer. 'The Death of Typography' became a running theme for Brody as he experimented with processes and pre-digital technologies, 'moving from type specimen book to photocopier, to graph paper and Rotring, pushing typographic forms into various distressed states'.[96]

Several of the typefaces in *Fuse*, such as Barry Deck's *Caustic Biomorph* and Tobias Frere-Jones' *Reactor*, became popular for display and poster work during the 1990s and a small number of *Fuse* fonts were included in the FontFont type library. The majority, however, (unless stored on hard disks) have disappeared as the original disks on which they were stored became unreadable. As a result, one of the era-defining projects of early digital typography is known solely through rare, highly collectable printed posters.

Whilst the headlines regarding magazines were that 'the future of communication was digital' the reality was that the influence of this new technology on the printed magazine industry was largely positive. Mark Porter, head of design at *The Guardian* newspaper, explained in 2000:

It has made it much cheaper to make sophisticated-looking magazines. Before the Macintosh [...] the only magazines that could afford to have sophisticated design were produced by big publishers with big art departments and a lot of investment in the production side of things. Where as nowadays it is possible to have a magazine published by someone in their front room. You can see it in the big

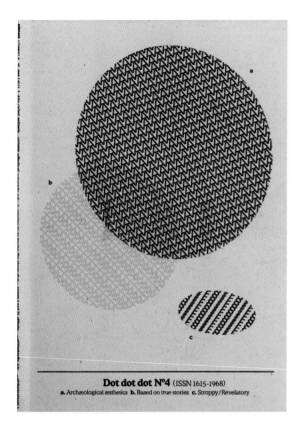

Dot dot dot Nº4 (ISSN 1615-1968)
a. Archæological æsthetics **b.** Based on true stories **c.** Stroppy/Revelatory

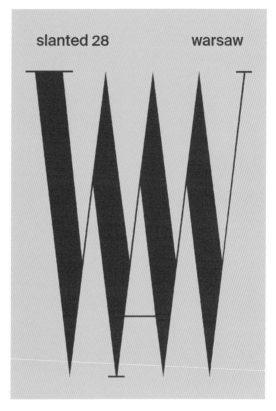

Above:
Dot Dot Dot, which described itself as 'not exactly a graphic design magazine', was edited and designed by Stuart Bailey and Peter Bil'ak. This small format magazine ran from 2001 to 2010 with a total of twenty published issues. Published in The Netherlands, text in English. This issue is from 2002.

Above right:
Slanted Magazine, launched 2005, is published in Germany, with text in English, each issue is 'mono-thematic and location based', covering graphic design, typography, illustration and photography. Edited and designed by Lars Harmsen and Julia Kahl.

publishers like Emap, they have got hundreds and hundreds of little sports magazines done with the kind of sophistication which even fifteen years ago would have seemed incredible.[97]

Porter's prediction proved correct. The number of independent magazines exploded, and continued to grow. Their distinctive diversity, coupled with high production values encouraged the establishment of specialist shops such as Athenaeum Nieuwscentrum Amsterdam and Magculture, London, exclusively to sell magazines. Jeremy Leslie, author and proprietor of Magculture explained: 'Distinct magazines, distinct worlds. And it's their physical differences that define those worlds. As soon as those worlds are squeezed on to an iPad they risk becoming the same.'[98]

Self-funded and often published just four to six times a year in small numbers (often less than 5,000) the founders of these independent magazines generally grew up with digital technology in their pocket. More lately, there has even been a hint of this in the coordination of images, white space and fewer words in these magazines of the random aesthetic sensibility of Tumblr and Pinterest. In other words, the Internet is coming off the screen and being printed onto paper.

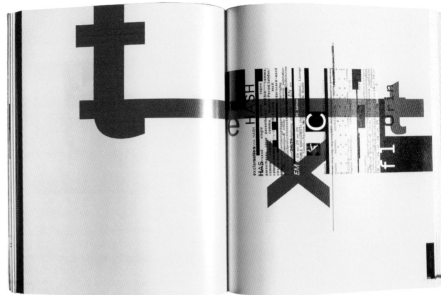

The

ce

pes

y

gns:

writing

r

ver

losely

on ·········stones.

t

o

m

b

general brillian
of Baskerville's ty
was influenced b
the copybook desi
he himself was a
master. Thei
actual forms howe
relate far more c
to those found

The english letter made its official a
ppearance in 1754 when the printer
, lettercutter, writing master and ja
panner *John Baskerville* began produ
cing his innovative letterforms: although t
here can be no doubt that his designs wer
e based on styles which had been develop
ed by tombstone carvers twenty or thirty
years previously. The clarendons, egyptian
s and **grotesques emerged from the
dense smoke of the Industrial Revo
lution round about 1800.** But long be
fore the first definitive forms appeared, m
any forms which now seem particularly E
nglish could be found in the primitive lett
erforms of early tombstones, builders' ma
rks and dates on houses, and even in Casl
on's types, derived though they were from
Dutch models.   Alan Bartram, quoted by Phil Baines

With g
, stron
ed thi
ong

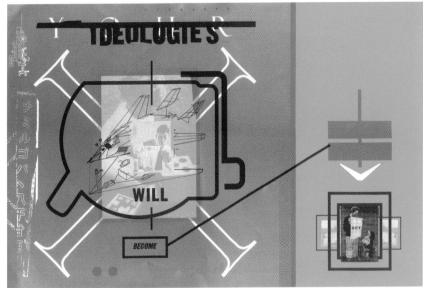

Opposite page, above left:
Phil Baines, Poster for 'Yak', 1994. This was one of
five posters published 'for fun and self-promotion', by
Why Not Associates. Other posters were designed
by Jonathan Barnbrook (opposite, above right) Andy
Altmann, David Ellis and Chris Priest on the theme
of their own influences.

Opposite page, above right:
Spread from *Typography Now: The Next Wave*,
designed by Why Not Associates, (Andy Altmann,
David Ellis and Howard Greenhalgh) London, 1991.

Opposite page, left:
Phil Baines, a page from the publication *Bound Image*,
by Phil Baines, David Blamey, Christopher Cook, David
Phillips, Jake Tilson & John Watson to accompany an
exhibition at Spacex Gallery, Exeter, UK, 1988.
  Baines, used a text by Alan Bartram concerning
English type designer and printer John Baskerville and
arranges it around a rubbing taken from an inscription
showing the origins of Baskerville's letterforms.

Above:
Why Not Associates, one of several divider pages
for a clothes catalogue for Next, the British clothing
company (1991).

Above right:
Jonathan Barnbrook, poster for 'Yak', 1994.
(See also Baines, opposite page, bottom left.)

The end of print (again)

Students leaving art college at the end of the 1980s were the first for whom digital technology was a standard design aid. But whilst its use may no longer have been contentious, it remained a relatively crude tool (compared with today's computers) requiring a steely determination to use. When Apple launched the Macintosh personal computer in 1984 its price was $2,500 (approximately £2,000). Software applications that came as part of the package included MacPaint, which made use of the mouse, and MacWrite, which demonstrated WYSIWYG (What You See Is What You Get) word processing and used a GUI (Graphic User Interface), although this was restricted to black and white. It also included MacDraw, a WYSIWYG vector graphic drawing application which, when used in conjunction with MacWrite demonstrated the possibilities of desktop publishing programs to come. Desktop printers such as the Apple Imagewriter (1984) and Apple LaserWriter (1985) offered black and white only.

The high cost of the Macintosh meant that even by the late 1980s a computer was still not the first item a fledgling design company required. When Andy Altmann, David Ellis and Howard Greenhalgh set up Why Not Associates in London in 1987 – straight after graduating from the RCA (Royal College of Art) – Altman explains that their studio consisted of:

> Just three drawing boards. David was teaching at the RCA at that time and he
> saw them buying the latest Apple computers. We decided we should invest in
> one. This would be around 1989. *The Next Directory* [a particularly high-profile
> commission at the time] and the Yak posters [opposite page and above] were
> designed on the computer but the type and other graphics were printed out by
> typesetters for us and then we artworked everything on drawing boards. It was
> a combination of old and new skills. We built a darkroom with a photographic

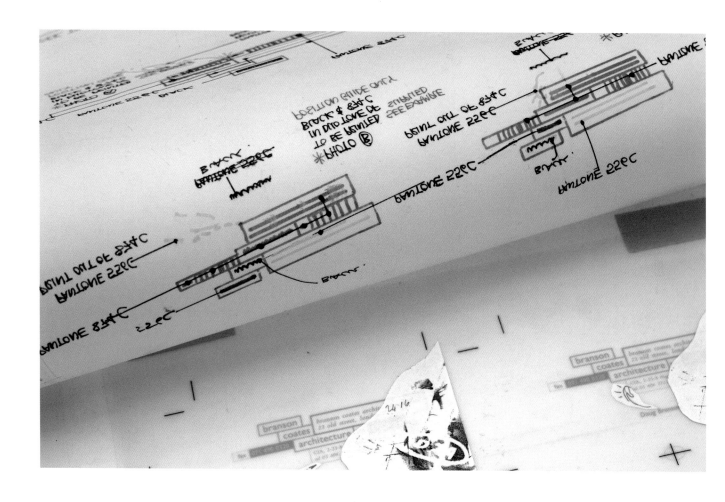

Above:
An example of hand-rendered artwork c.1989.
This artwork, designed and produced by Why Not
Associates for Branson Coates Architecture, consists
of a sheet of CS10 Artboard (or lineboard) on which
cut-out photoset type has been pasted down, and
an overlay of tracing paper on which photographic
material for a second colour has also been pasted.
The purpose of the third and final overlay is to convey
information to the printer regarding colours and
paper stock to be used.

enlarger and a PMT camera. We would get the typesetter to print out our files
from the Mac and then enlarge, distort and play with them in the darkroom
and then put it all together on art board in layers on the drawing board.
Aldus PageMaker (from 1985) was a huge improvement and became the DTP software
of choice for many professional designers until the arrival of QuarkXPress 3.3 in
1992. This, the fifth version of QuarkXPress (the first having being introduced in
1987) together with Adobe PhotoShop, which had been launched in 1988, would,
finally, cause the demise of the PMT camera.

Why Not Associates and fellow graduates of the RCA Phil Baines and Jonathan
Barnbrook, were all given generous international exposure by VanderLans' through
Emigre, but this also caused them to be lumped rather awkwardly with American
typographers such as Anne Burdick, Barry Deck, Edward Fella, Robert Nakata etc.
But it was another American graphic designer, who arrived unannounced in the
early 1990s and circumvented every recognised design institution to become (or so
it seemed) every graphic design student's favourite designer: David Carson.

A sociology undergraduate and former professional surfer with little formal
design education, Carson established his international reputation when he designed
a six-issue run of the magazine *Beach Culture* following which, in 1992, he became

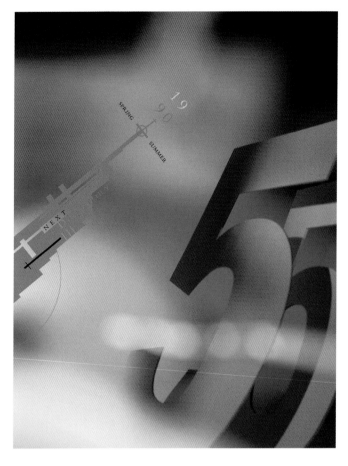

art director of the music media magazine *Ray Gun*, established by its founding editor Neil Feineman in Santa Monica, California as a competitor to *Rolling Stone*.

Ray Gun occurred at the moment print media was thought to be facing its putative demise. Carson's magazine spreads, including orchestrated 'chaotic', degraded or damaged texts and images, had a sense of the apocalyptic about them. Indeed, Carson encouraged this interpretation by including as the tag line 'The End of Print' on later covers.[99] (One of Carson's tag lines on the cover of *Beach Culture* had been 'The End of Summer'.) The absence of a grid structure; no cohesion in graphic style; no page numbers or running heads; no standardised hierarchy of information; and especially the free-form approach on spread after spread, was achieved, as Carson explains, by the first six issues being designed without recourse to computers or DTP software '...I was starting with a blank layout board – no guidelines or snap-to grids, no document structure, no pre-set page number placement etc. Nothing fixed, standardized, formatted [...] The time-frame was as long as we had, 24/7, to get it done. It was never about the money, of which there was barely any.'[100]

Whilst the design process would, over time, be transformed by digital technology, the appearance and, to a large extent, the content of *Ray Gun* remained an extension of Carson's own distinctive personality. In this way, the body of graphic design work

Opposite page:
Detail from an advertisement for *The End of Print: The Grafik Design of David Carson,* published by Chronicle Books, 1995.

associated with Carson's *Ray Gun* in the last decade of the 20th century has come to epitomise the ability of print media to assimilate, contain and usurp the threat of new media.

The significance of *Ray Gun* was that it not only re-established the (apparently) tenuous state of print media's hold on the cultural imagination, but that it also drew on the massive reserves of economic power and material attraction still vested in print – altogether, a complex but entertaining and controversial apotheosis rather than anything so convenient as the 'end of print'. Indeed, *Ray Gun* was a powerful demonstration of print's capacity not only to emulate and even celebrate cultural aspects of new media but, remarkably, also consolidate an aesthetic identity for digital media. Print media was never threatened by David Carson – quite the opposite, it was celebrated.

global graphic takeover

new essays by
~~david bowie, william~~ gibson,
~~michael stipe~~ and

~~r.e.m. designer chris bilheimer, ray gun~~
~~managing editor dean kuipers,~~
~~magazine editor rick poynor and ray gun~~
~~lisher marvin scott jarrett, plus~~
~~the best of~~
~~ray gun interviews~~

book of design, illustration, photography,
action,
and style that matters

ray
gun

culture

rAy
gUn™
OUT OF
ONTRO

What Your Music Looks Like

Graphic remixes by   In Bookstores   SIMON
Chris Ashworth,   SCHUST
                                               EDITION

Below:
Horace Hart, *Rules for Compositors and Readers at the University Press Oxford*, popularly known as 'Hart's Rules' in the print industry. First published in 1893 and still in print today, this is the 1952 edition.

Bottom:
Opening page of *A Dictionary of Printing Terms*, published by Linotype & Machinery Ltd, 1962.

Below:
John Lewis and John Brinkley, book cover, *Graphic Design: Lettering, typography and illustration*, published by Routledge & Kegan Paul, 1954. This book represents the content of one of the earliest courses to be called 'graphic design', established in 1949 by Lewis and Brinkley at the Royal College of Art, London.

Opposite page:
Cover, *Monotype Book of Information*, published by the Monotype Corporation, c. 1968.

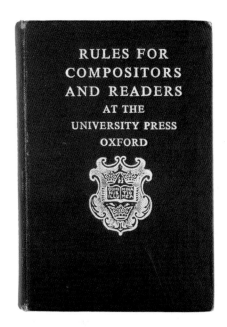

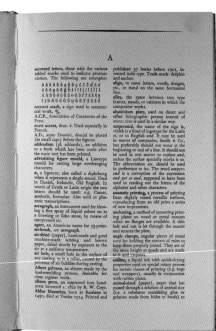

Chapter 9:
Transmutations

Terminal printed casualties?

There are certain characteristics that printed items under severe threat from digital technology have in common: they tend to hold a vast quantity of information that must be regularly updated in order to function whilst their unavoidable volume makes reprinting expensive.

The telephone directory is a prime example. It was an intrinsic tool that had a presence in every house, office, shop and school in almost every country. Its pervasive presence ensured that everyone from a very early age became familiar with its distinctive page layout and learnt how to use it. Every country had its own, deftly different way of organising precisely the same information and these small differences came to represent something akin to a national identity.

The function of all reference books, including directories, catalogues, atlases, lexicons, dictionaries and encyclopædias, is to be consulted while doing something else. The mid 20th century printer's 'reference' shelf would include one of the standard dictionaries plus *Roget's Thesaurus*, *The Oxford Dictionary of Quotations*, and *Fowler's Modern English Usage*, or their equivalents – all essential aids in the composition of type. In addition, the compositor would have a recent copy of *Hart's Rules for Compositors and Readers at the University Press, Oxford*, small enough to be discreetly kept in a pocket but essential for typographic and/or grammatical reference. Elsewhere in the printworks would be numerous catalogues for papers, inks, adhesives, ancillary tools and equipment plus a number of well-thumbed voluminous type specimen books.

By the 1960s there might be families without a dictionary or the need for a telephone directory, yet it was likely there would be a set of encyclopædias. Such was the allure of these books that many parents felt duty-bound to buy a set as an essential aid for their children's general knowledge and well-being.

The encyclopædia reinvented

Nothing better demonstrates the inherent characteristics marking both print and digital technology than the changing fortunes of the encyclopædia (a story that runs roughly parallel with that of the dictionary). *Chambers' Cyclopaedia, or Universal Dictionary of Arts and Sciences* (1728), and the *Encyclopédie of Denis Diderot and Jean le Rond d'Alembert* (from 1751 onwards) established the form that would still be recognized today: a comprehensive range of topics, discussed in depth and organized in an accessible, systematic method.

The first edition of the *Encyclopædia Britannica*, published in Edinburgh from 1768, appeared in weekly instalments, the second edition, from 1777, took the now familiar form of a set of substantial volumes with topics organised in alphabetical order. In the earliest editions most of the entries were written by its editor William Smellie, but the publishing enterprise was soon profitable enough for prominent scholars to be commissioned to write entries on their own specialities. A national institution had been established.

The scale of such an undertaking is remarkable and yet the *Encyclopædia Britannica* continued to grow until, by the end of the 20th century, it required around 100 full-time editors and more than 4,000 contributors. The last printed version (in 2010) ran to 32 volumes and 32,640 pages. The world's largest Encyclopædia, however, was the Spanish *Enciclopedia Universal Ilustrada Europeo-Americana* (published serially in 118 volumes between 1908 to 1930).[101]

By the late 20th century, encyclopædias were already being published on CD-ROMS for use with personal computers. Microsoft's *Encarta*, launched in 1993, was also an important landmark because it was the first to have no printed equivalent.[102]

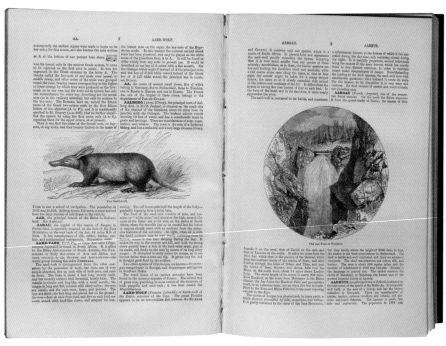

Topics were supplemented with video and audio files as well as numerous images. Britannica's executives initially considered the CD−ROM encyclopædia as an irrelevance: a child's toy. In this case their reaction was understandable. Microsoft had licensed the text for *Encarta* from *Funk & Wagnalls*, whose encyclopædia, first published in 1912, was barely surviving as a periodic promotional item in American supermarkets. The addition of public-domain illustrations and poor quality sound recordings that were too old to bear a copyright hardly seemed serious enough to be considered a rival. But when Microsoft discontinued *Encarta* in 2009, the reason for its demise was not the poor quality of its content, nor was it an improved *Encyclopædia Britannica*. Something new had emerged – Wikipedia.

Opposite page:
The National Encyclopædia, spine and typical spread, UK, 1910 edition. Particular attention was paid to the design of the spine of encyclopedias. It was important that collectively they communicated authority but also appeared contemporary. Internally, colour was rarely used, the paper thin and the text densely set; all features that conveyed a sense that the information was essential, plentiful, and without embellishment.

Right:
Advertisement for *The World Book Encyclopedia,* USA, 1965.

In 2010, after 224 years (and just nine years after Wikipedia) the last printed edition of *Encyclopædia Britannica* appeared and its subscription-based digital version was launched two years later. Changes were immediately apparent. Its President, Jorge Cauz, explained in an interview at the time,

> The digital environment allows for a process that is intrinsically cooperative, which is the creation and dissemination of knowledge. So users can suggest content, links, bibliographies, for entries. Suggestions will be vetted to make sure they're correct. [...] We have only accepted 33% of user submissions and they helped enlarge the database, made it more accurate, and pointed out different ways to treat a topic and areas where we needed to expand knowledge.'[103]

The enduring status of *Encyclopædia Britannica* was based on the fact that entries were written by experts in their field, whose scholarship helped to recruit other eminent figures to contribute. The ninth (1902) edition is considered a high point in international scholarship and literary style. However, when faced with a catastrophic fall in sales, Encyclopædia Britannica Incorporated (the company became American-owned in 1920) transferred its encyclopædia from paper to screen, and decided to seek volume at the sacrifice of recognised authority.

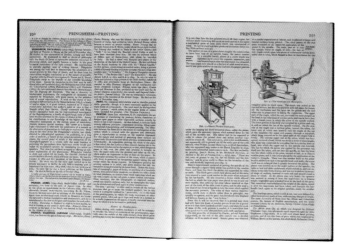
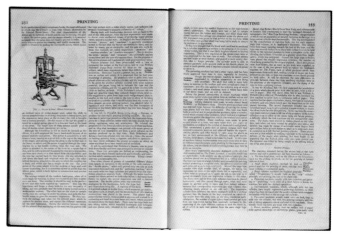
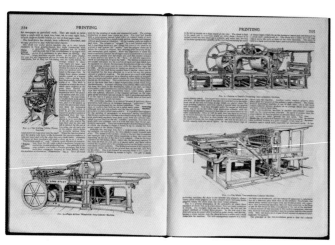
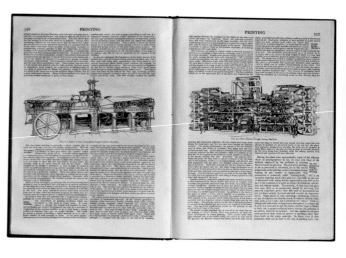

Opposite page and below:
Encyclopædia Britannica, 1910 edition and (below) the current online version. In the 1910 edition the topic 'Printing' required the equivlent of eight pages, some 8,000 words and nine detailed illustrations. The same topic in the current online *Encyclopædia Britannica* has an initial 300-word description, two images (the three other blanked-out images are advertisements) whose purpose are largely decorative, and several links – 'ink' and 'paper' for example – each providing similar 'bite-size' amounts of information and, again, containing further links. In this way, the information route is driven by the reader rather than the expertise of an author.

Below right:
Wikipedia logo, 2016. Wikipedia was launched in 2001 by Jimmy Wales and Larry Sanger.

The editors of printed encyclopædias have always been faced with the problem of what to discard (often valuable material of historic nature) to make room for the enormous annual amount of new material. With each new issue editors took pride in producing the most up-to-date encyclopædia possible whilst simultaneously working on the next 'updated' edition.

The transient nature of knowledge lends itself to digital technology. This is something that was recognised by Jimmy Wales and Larry Sanger when they launched Wikipedia in 2001: a corroboratively edited, multilingual, free Internet encyclopædia. Its success has been a phenomenon: as of March 2016, it had 5,113,307 articles in the English Wikipedia alone (and there are 286 other language editions worldwide). However, that a digital encyclopædias in itself might be a successful proposition is far less surprising than the premise that its content should be based almost entirely on unsolicited and anonymous contributors.

As a result, not all Wikipedia pages are alike in quality. The more popular a topic is, the more scrutiny it gets from Wikipedia editors. In a sense, all Wikipedia topics are works in progress and with credibility always in flux. The editors generally mark incomplete or unreviewed pages as 'stubs', and place warning labels on pages that may be biased or prone to vandalism. Many academics, historians and journalists recommend caution when using Wikipedia, indeed, some universities banned students from citing Wikipedia and others have blocked campus network access. Such measures have been criticized and the term 'luddite' predictably called. This is understandable because Wikipedia's own guidelines, together with the statements of its founders, advise against using Wikipedia as anything other than a tertiary source for information. Students incapable of taking advice, the argument goes, have every right to fail (as well as succeed) in their studies.

The size of Wikipedia was graphically demonstrated by the New York artist Michael Mandiberg who wrote software that enabled him to transform and print the entire English language Wikipedia as it existed 7 April, 2015. Titled *Print Wikipedia*,[104] it required 7,473 volumes each consisting of 700 pages. The list of contributors alone (a legal requirement) required sixteen volumes. The upload process took a little over twenty-four days and the printing costs of one complete set is estimated to be $500,000.

The resurrection of the type specimen book

Because type foundries' promotional material was aimed almost exclusively at the printing profession the standard of its design and the quality of printing and finishing was often excellent, sometimes innovative. Such material has become increasingly important – and scarce – to those interested in the history of printing, typography and graphic design, but none more so than the type specimen book. Type specimen books arrived in all shapes and sizes. Those with a complete range of types and ancillary materials from a major type foundry were generally casebound (see page 115) and could have many hundreds of pages. One of the biggest, *Die Hauptprobe* from the German type foundry D Stempel AG published 1925, had 1,200 pages. But they could also be a modestly slim stapled booklet, or even a single sheet displaying a single typeface. The purpose of these documents was to persuade the printer to buy new fonts (then 'founts') – never a cheap or simple decision. Initially, foundries set about this task simply and rationally, by displaying every character (upper and lowercase, small caps, accented letters, numerals, punctuation, ligatures,

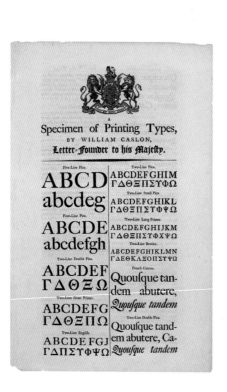

Opposite page, left:
William Caslon's *A Specimen of Printing Types*, 1785. Cover of an eight-page display of types and borders printed by Galabin & Baker of London for insertion into copies of *Chamber's Cyclopaedia*.

Opposite page, right:
Eric Gill's *Gill Sans*, commissioned by Stanley Morrison, typographic advisor to the Monotype Corporation and completed in 1928, used here to promote the company's product and font range.

Below:
Page from *Memphis Schriften*, published by the German type foundry, D Stempel AG, 1938.

as well as typographic, mathematical and scientific symbols) of a given font and then repeating exactly the same display of characters for each size and weight of the fount available. They might also provide a sample setting – a short paragraph perhaps – of each.

But as the Industrial Revolution began to take hold the purpose of type *and* of printing began to change. Printing was no longer concerned primarily with books but with an ever-broadening range of printing services – including labels and packaging, posters and leaflets, stationery and business cards, certificates and legal documents etc. Commercial imperatives demanded that the 19th century type specimen book took account of these functions, both in the typefaces they were offering and in the manner in which they were displayed.

A printer's training focused on the way typography functioned in bookwork and so was ill-prepared for the more eclectic requirements of, for example, advertising, packaging or poster work. To help the printer, foundries displayed these fonts in a way that also demonstrated the function for which they were designed. In this way,

Below:
Divertissements Typographiques number 1, art directed by Maximilien Vox, Deberny & Peignot type foundry, Paris, 1928. *Divertissements Typographiques* comprised of loose sheets of professional graphic work chosen to show Deberny & Peignot fonts at their best.

type specimen books also became graphic design manuals for the printer before graphic design was conceived as a separate profession.[105]

The 1920s was the period when the largest and most impressive of the type specimen books appeared. From this point onward alternative ways of promoting new typefaces began being explored – lighter, less cumbersome type specimen documents whose authority was established by design rather than by weight and volume. The 1920s was also the decade that type foundries began to swap allegiances, from the printer to the designer. Foundries such as Deberny & Peignot in Paris engaged with the ambitious nature of the design profession with the publication of *Les Divertissements Typographiques*, which was part type specimen book, part showcase and part magazine. Designed by Maximilien Vox and first published in 1928, it took the form of a folder that held a number of carefully chosen examples of real graphic work. Apart from being judged to be of a high standard of design and print, all had to include fonts by Deberny & Peignot.

Although *Les Divertissements Typographiques* was sent free of charge to printers who stocked Deberny & Peignot's fonts, it was also distributed to advertising agencies and design consultancies in the sure knowledge that designers would also want to see their own work presented in the 'journal' and, therefore, more likely to specify Deberny & Peignot's fonts. At roughly the same time, Charles Peignot, head of Deberny & Peignot, also created and edited the journal *Arts et Métiers Graphiques*,

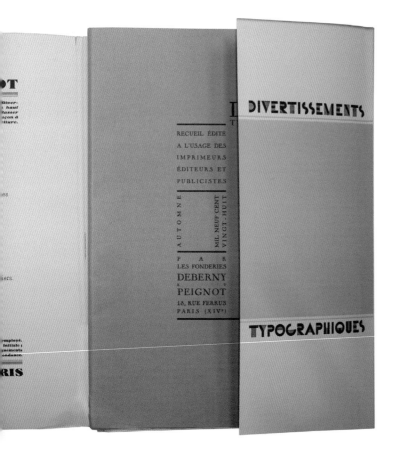
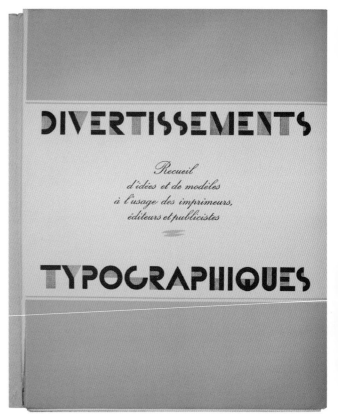

Right:

A page from the Curwen Press *Newsletter*, a regular publication, typically restrained in character, sent to clients, advertising agencies and graphic designers to showcase recent work and additions to their type catalogue, 1935.

Far right:

Cover of *ITC Caslon*, published by the International Typographic Company, New York. This is one of a celebrated series of leaflets, each devoted to a different typeface and all characterised by the use of bright colours. The tight setting is typical of the period and *ITC Caslon*, especially in the USA, was particularly prone to this aberration.

Below:

Jeremy Tankard, leaflet showing *Capline,* an all-cap display font designed in 2010 (published 2013) using FontLab, Cambridge, UK.

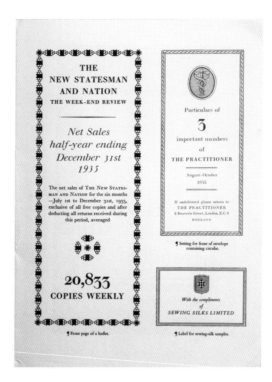
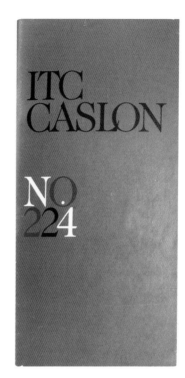

An all capital typeface with an inline detail that varies in width. The fonts that comprise Capline have the same outside shape and share the same spacing. This allows the designer to layer the different fonts to achieve a variety of effects.

The change to the inline gives the impression of a change in weight. As the inline becomes thinner, the fonts appear to become heavier. The Heavy font has a thin inline, whereas the Thin font has a heavy inline. Or are the lighter fonts in outline?

When does inline become outline?

Beautifully engineered with wide proportions and generous curves. Capline has a strong personality and a crisp, clean, elegant feel that makes it an ideal typeface for editorial, display and branding purposes.

one of the earliest journals to focus on graphic design but which also featured allied subjects such as illustration, photography, the history of the book, and the expanding disciplines of advertising design, as well as new printing techniques. The journal also featured regular reviews of fine limited-edition books as well as examples of innovative typographic layouts. Each edition was printed on high-quality papers and often including tipped-in plates and inserts. The Second World War forced the journal to close.

Peignot was scathing about the lack of typographic culture and curiosity in the printing and publishing worlds. However, there were certainly some printing companies who were fully aware, if not entirely appreciative of new ideas and developments toted by those within the graphic design fraternity. The manufacture of typesetting equipment by companies such as Monotype and Linotype enabled larger printing enterprises to produce their own type from matrixes. As a consequence, printing companies would publish their own periodic updates in the form of newsletters, brochures and, occasionally, even their own company type specimen catalogues for regular clients. Such publications not only displayed the range of fonts currently held – a major criterion for a designer choosing a printer – but also an excuse for them to demonstrate their skills and inventive ambition in composition and presswork.

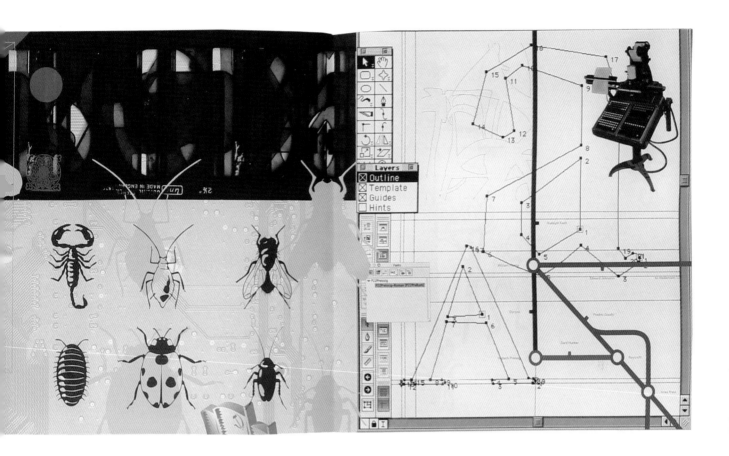

Opposite page top:
Double-page spread with fold-outs from one of
P22's numerous examples of material celebrating
their typefaces in print. Such material arrives in
many forms, including pocket-size booklets, playing
cards and packaged CDs, all distinguished by their
inventive use of papers and printing technologies.

Opposite page, bottom:
Cover, *Notes on the Design of DTL Valiance Cyrillic*,
from the Dutch Type Library, s-Hertogenbosch,
The Netherlands.

Right:
Cover, *Catalogue of Typefaces*, (fifth edition) from
Hoefler & Co, New York.

The best printer's specimens not only displayed typefaces, but also provided technical information such as character set or casting-off tables; in effect, a technical manual of typography for the designer in its content and presentation.

Despite the development of phototypesetting, it was the digital revolution in the 1980s that brought the great type founding dynasties to an end. Since the future was now digital and the end of print presumed inevitable, the idea of promoting digital typefaces using print was, understandably, an anathema. By the early 2000s, every digital type foundry was displaying and selling typefaces directly via the Web, supported by e-newsletters and samples downloadable as PDFs. One of the last, and largest, type specimen books was published by FontShop (co-owned by Neville Brody and Erik Spiekermann) in 2009.

Nevertheless, today, few digital foundries have no printed material at all, although the form it might take is unpredictable: anything from posters to postcards, primers to pamphlets. And many, for example Emigre and P22 in the USA, and Jeremy Tankard Typography in the UK, use print prodigiously. The luscious appeal of letter-forms printed with care onto paper makes such specimens impossible to discard. Plus, as Tankard explains:

> Print is social, interactive, whilst a screen is one dimensional. There is something very satisfying about designing and producing a printed item. So much can be achieved from the choice of papers, the use of special colours and techniques, designing the pace and rhythm across pages, the feel and sound of the paper, the play of light, size, shape. Even smell. The production of printed samples is also therapeutic after the hours of computer production. It reminds me of what type is for.' [106]

Fontstand

Fonts   Pricing   Students   Gift Cards   Articles   Blog   iOS App   Recommend   Help   E-mail Newsl

↓ Download 1.3.0

Mac OS X 10.9 and newer
6.2 MB

One-click font rentals for desktop and web.

Fontstand is a Mac OS X app that allows you to ~~try~~ fonts for free or rent them by the month for de~~sktop~~ and web use for just a fraction of the regular pr~~ice~~

Choose from 1025 families from 43 foundries ›

 Introduction

~~T~~ry fonts for free in any app

~~Y~~ou can try fonts for free. ~~T~~hey will be activated on ~~y~~our computer for 1 hour.

Rent fonts just for 10% of their price

You can rent fonts for 10% of their retail price per month and use them as you would any regular font.

Share fonts with co-workers

Share fonts with your team for just a fraction of the rental price.

Easy-to-use webfonts

Most of the fonts include also free, hosted, easy-to-set up webfonts.

Keep fo~~nts~~

After you've ~~rented~~ a total of 1~~2 months it'll~~ be yours ~~to keep~~ f~~orever~~

~~Prod~~uction Type
~~3~~7 families 190 fonts

Letters from Sweden
13 families 80 fonts

Emigre
101 families 520 fonts

Rosetta
24 families 186 fonts

Blackletra
8 families 58 fonts

~~B~~old
~~M~~onday

Bold Monday

Commercial

Commercial Type

OHNO

OH no Type Co.

newlyn

newlyn

TypeTogether

Below:
Michael Harvey cut these majestic capitals on the staircase of the National Gallery Sainsbury Wing, London, in 1989. Perhaps not surprisingly the stone-work, where accessible, is stained by fingers exploring the texture left by Harvey's chisel.

Below right:
Detail from a sign designed and cast in metal to adorn the side of a train c. 1910.

Opposite page:
A2/SW/HK (Scott Williams and Henrik Kubel) London. Book cover design with bespoke typefaces for Penguin Books, New York, 2005–2006. The specially drawn letters incorporate a debossing process to provide the paper cover with a reference to the valued permanence proffered by stone or metal.

Since the digital revolution, the physical presence of the book has been given a great deal more emphasis by the resurrection of ancillary print processes often developed by the Victorian printer.

Chapter 10:
Celebrating the limitations of print

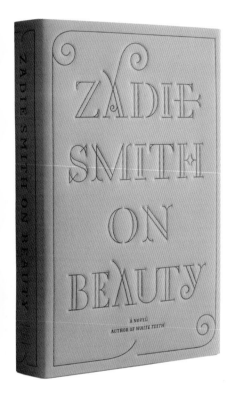

The diverse characteristics of print

Since the launch of the e-reader, there has been a genuine reappraisal of paper and print, type and typography, and more specifically, the craft skills essential in making these different elements and processes work so well. Why is this the case? Indeed, why does print still exist?

Whilst limitless possibilities were apparently on offer with digital technology it has become increasingly evident that, paradoxically, it is the parameters, the physical limitations of printed paper, that encourages an inventive outlook. Indeed, fascination in the physicality of print – take for example, paper: the various ways it can feel, its weight, volume, surface area, shape and edges, and the various ways it can be scored, folded, perforated, and bound – has become increasingly important as designers and a more confident publishing industry seeks to emphasise the differences between print and pixel. This, in turn, has renewed interest in paper making, a two-thousand year old craft, and a product that only recently was described as extinct.

The 'semantics of the page' was once regarded as being concerned solely with the words printed on it.[107] However, during the last twenty years, perhaps in response to the emergence of e-readers, semantic study now recognises that the meaning of a text is carried not only by words but also by the physical and material features of the page itself. This includes printing processes, choice of typeface, its arrangement and position on the page, compositional design of margins, gutter, inter-line and inter-column spaces. The 'supplementary' textual material often offered on the title page and cover, as well as the colophon offers copious syntactic material. Also acknowledged is the importance of other sensory attributes previously ignored such as the weight, shape and binding of the document, the characteristics of the papers used, and even issues such as the perceived and real costs and relative rarity of the document.

That the material form of a printed document – how and with what it was made – influences the initial impression and ultimate meaning by the reader, will not be a surprise to typographers or graphic designers. The sheer diversity of physical surfaces and containers onto which printed words can and have been applied or contained, especially since the Industrial Revolution, is endless. Such materials: their choice, manipulation and subsequent use, play an essential role in establishing a printed text's 'aura' – that special quality held by all unique artefacts that Walter Benjamin, in *The Work of Art in the Age of Mechanical Reproduction*, argued was lost in subsequent reincarnations.

Benjamin's extended essay explored the concept of authenticity: 'Even the most perfect reproduction of a work of art is lacking in one element: its presence in time and space, its unique existence at the place where it happens to be'.[108] Similarly, the reason that a book from a first edition is often sought after is because it brings the reader into contact with the author's own particular time and place, achieved by the authentic materials, and methods and processes of its making and printing. It will even have its own smell and particular feel in the hand as the cover is lifted and its pages parted.

Subsequent editions evoke a different resonance, another time, place and attitude. That an author's words can take on a new, perhaps even alternative aspect by the choice and arrangement of type printed on different paper between different covers demonstrates the subtle cultural nuances of print and its associated materials. Resonance, or 'aura', is not limited to individual items, or even 'limited' print runs, some of the most iconic *and* ambitious publishing events have been series

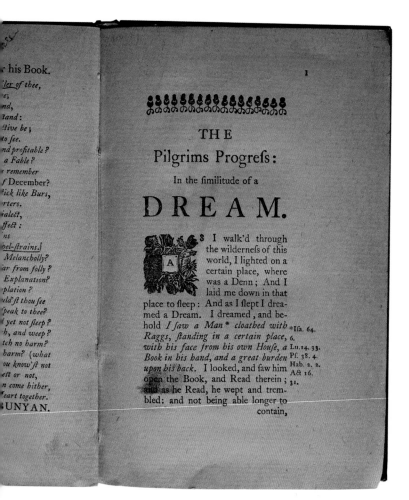

or 'imprints' in terms of both volume and scope. The harnessing of electric power in the second half of the 19th century enabled publishers to think on a huge scale. And with increased scale came influence and social responsibility, something some took very seriously – others less so. The subject of these early famous series was, predominantly, the 'classic' novel, crucially, out of copyright and so freely available. In each case, although the texts themselves remain the same, their alternate guise, – fated to be influenced by the popular cultural style of another time, – anchor each to their new times and places.

The popular printed novel

One of the first publishers to attempt a large-scale literary series was J M Dent & Company, London, which began its Everyman's Library in 1906: a remarkably ambitious one thousand pocket-sized, classic titles following the design principles and style established by William Morris in his Kelmscott Press some seventeen years earlier.

Right:
J M Dent's Temple Shakespeare series was begun in 1894 and its success enabled Dent to launch the Everyman Library. Illustration by Eric Gill.

Opposite page, left:
Cover of *Die Minnesinger in Bildern der Manessischen Handschrift*, from the popular Insel Bücherei (Island Library) series published by Insel Verlag and printed by Pöeschel & Trepte, Leipzig, Germany, c. 1930s. The card covers offered substantial protection.

Opposite page, right:
Penguin tri-band paperback cover, 1937. Although ostensibly a travel book this is one of several books published by Penguin in the run-up to the Second World War concerning what might be described as 'British' values.

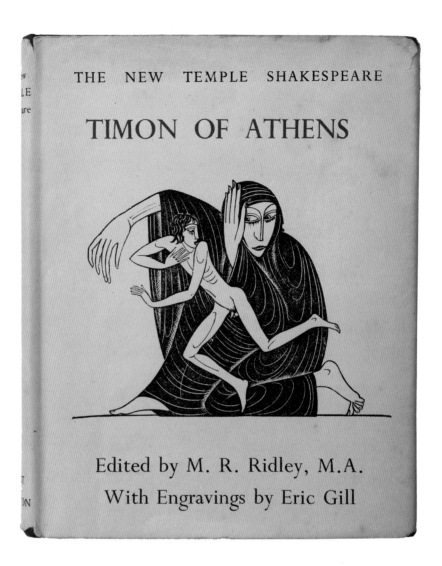

Since 1889, Dent had built a reputation for publishing beautiful books, usually printed in small runs on handmade paper, with illustrations from, among others, Aubrey Beardsley, Walter Crane and Eric Gill, and in 1894 published the highly successful Temple Shakespeare series. But the concept and scale of the Everyman Library was unprecedented – as was their bargain value. Despite the high quality of the materials and binding, new and faster printing technology enabled Dent to sell these books for just one shilling (or 5p). The first of the series was Boswell's *Life of Johnson*, which had a quotation by John Milton on the title page: 'A good book is the precious life-blood of a master-spirit, embalmed and treasured upon purpose to a life beyond life'. Dent's aim was to publish new and beautiful editions of the world's classics so that 'for a few shillings the reader may have a whole bookshelf of the immortals; for five pounds (which will procure him a hundred volumes) a man may be intellectually rich for life'. The range of the series was also impressive although novels of 'dubious morals', *Moll Flanders* for example,

were excluded. Dent did not live to see the one thousandth volume which was printed in 1956.

Insel Verlag ('Island Publishing House') in Leipzig launched its Insel Bücherei ('Island Library') in 1912. It was initiated by Anton Kippenberg, concentrating initially on classic German texts, hand-set and printed (using a Fraktur typeface) by Pöeschel & Trepte in Leipzig, whose new young co-director, Carl Ernst Poeschel was a member of the German Werkbund. The most striking feature of The Island series (which cost 50 Pfennig, about 6p) was Kippenberg's decision to use rich, brightly coloured patterned papers to cover the boards onto which a label bearing the title and author was pasted.

The provenance of these papers – originally printed from woodblocks by the Italian family company of Remondini between 1634 and 1861 – seemed to validate the idea that traditional and modern values could be one and the same. The books were generally kept quite slim, and Kippenberg involved leading artists and designers of

Below:
Spicy Mystery Stories, *The Executioner,* August
1935, published by the Culture Publications Inc,
Delaware, USA.

Below right:
Random House's Everyman's Library, newly launched
in 1991, in their new livery (2017) and printed on
acid-free paper.

the day, such as Eric Gill, Rudolf Koch, Emil Preetorius and Henry van de Velde in their design.

Insel Bücherei was a huge success, both critically and financially – in the first two years a million copies were sold. This publishing phenomenon, incorporating high printing standards, carefully crafted typography and attractively designed covers, was much discussed in publishing trade journals everywhere, and especially in England.

Penguin Books was founded in 1935 by Allen Lane and revolutionised publishing through its lowly priced paperbacks (sold for six pence, or 2.5p) and by their use of unconventional outlets such as Woolworths (Lane considered the traditional bookshop too formal). Covers consisted of a simple horizontal grid using colours to signify the genre of each book: orange for fiction, green for crime, blue for biography etc.

The company became a national institution during the Second World War with erudite yet bestselling books such as Harold Nicolson's *Why Britain is at War*, and down-to-earth manuals such as *Aircraft Recognition* and *Keeping Poultry and Rabbits on Scraps*. As well as its broad range of classic fiction titles, Penguin also published books on politics, the arts and science, and in so doing played a major role in the establishment of critical public debate. Indeed, their simple design, complete with Gill's sans serif typeface on their covers, came to epitomise the strife and rationing of the war years. After the war Jan Tschichold was invited to be Penguin's Design Director and between 1947 and 1949 he added an intellectually rigorous visual language to all of Penguin Books' publications.

The concept of American 'pulp fiction' was also established during the Second World War. American troops, like their British counterparts, received free paperback books – texts packed into double-columns, trimmed to a size that could be easily slipped into the uniform pocket, and with the expectation that it would be thrown away after use. But the reading habit established between long periods of inaction continued after the war and, in 1947, some ninety-five million paperback books were sold in the United States. Paperbacks changed the book business in America in much the same way that the forty-five rpm 'single' vinyl record, introduced in 1949, and the transistor radio in 1954, changed the music industry by making the product cheaply and plentiful.

However, unlike Penguin and Insel Verlag, American paperback publishers such as Pocket Books, New American Library and Spicy Mystery Stories established a marketing policy that was deliberately downmarket. Pocket Books' Robert de Graff explained: 'These new Pocket Books are [...] as handy as a pencil, as modern and convenient as a portable radio'. He viewed his books as being disposable – more akin to a newspaper or magazine than a book. In the years between the end of the war in 1945 and the introduction of television during the early 1950s, pulp fiction met this basic need. Kurt Enoch, co-founder, with Victor Weybridge, of New American Library expressed a similar view: 'There is real hope for a culture that makes it as easy to buy a book as it does a pack of cigarettes'.[109] Sold alongside newspapers, superhero comics and lurid 'true detective' magazines, pulp fiction covers were unashamedly designed to compete on equal terms.

There is little mention of philanthropic motives from de Graf or Enoch. However, since they were willing to publish anything that might turn a profit they made no distinction whatsoever between, for example, Emily Brontë and Mickey Spillane, and used the same cover designs and illustration style for both. And it worked. In the same year that New American Library published Spillane's debut novel, *I, the Jury* (1947) it also published reprints of books by James Joyce, William Faulkner, Thomas Wolfe and Arthur Koestler, whilst the Pocket Books' edition of Emily Brontë's *Wuthering Heights* hit the best-seller list with over 1.5 million paperback copies being sold. Pulp fiction as an idea was not so much in the writing as in its design, marketing and distribution.

Today, pulp fiction cover art and their creators, such as James Avati and Rudolph Belarski, are celebrated in exhibitions and, of course, in books. Similarly, there have

Below left:
A 'used' Kindle e-reader: 'state of the art' digital technology whose screen saver displays an image of a typewriter. Other Kindle screen savers depict letterpress wood characters and an old elaborate dip pen and ink well.

Below right:
A used book: printed books have a generosity of spirit that is integral to their form and function, regardless of age. They continue to give by displaying their covers, even when, as with this 118-year-old book, the title has been rubbed off. (Actually, it is *Advertise! How? When? Where?* by W Smith.) Age is not a barrier: indeed the attraction proffered by the worn covered boards and the feathered edges of its pages only add to its allure.

been numerous publications celebrating the cultural importance of Penguin's paperbacks and, perhaps to a lesser degree, the Everyman's Library and Insel Bücherei.

Such publishing achievements have come to represent the period in which their books were produced and, for their owners such books possess emotional resonance. Despite their initial low intrinsic value their place on many people's book shelves and in public archives – as well as increasing in second-hand value – suggests that their power, or 'aura', is indeed as much to do with their own physical manifestation as the author's words they carry. The book itself also tells a story.

In every case, the characteristics that distinguish one book from the next and one publisher from another are created by the graphic designer and typographer – often one and the same person. Dent commissioned Reginald Knowles to design his Everyman's Library, a task later taken over by Eric Ravilious, although in both cases the textual material was handled by Dent's compositors at his Temple Press. The design of Insel Verlag's 'Island Library' was directed by Anton Kippenberg and undertaken with care by the compositors at Carl Ernst Poeschel's printing company. The initial design of the Penguin Book covers was established by the then twenty-one-year-old office junior Edward Young, and the texts set by various printing companies to various standards. But after the war Jan Tschichold brought a new

Below:
Leather 'covers' for the Amazon Kindle, not only providing 'the feel of a luxuriously bound book' but also enables the reader to open and hold their e-reader like the real thing.

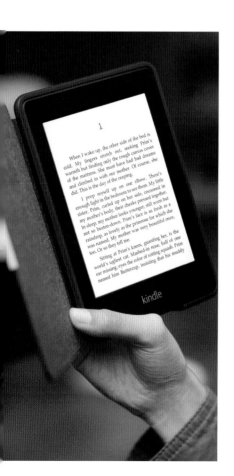

order to Penguin's books and, as such, became one of the first designers to also take responsibility for *all* typographic aspects, including textual material, for which he wrote and had printed a four page 'Penguin Composition Rules' to ensure consistency in, for example, word spacing, paragraph indents, punctuation, figures, capitals, small caps, etc for commissioned printers to follow. Other typographic design illuminaries such as Hans Schmoller and Germano Facetti followed Tschichold's accomplished tenure at Penguin.

Today, whilst the 'Penguin Classics' series continues with great success, and the Everyman Library has been elegantly relaunched by Random House, the first decade of the 21st century will undoubtedly be remembered as the era of the 'downloadable' novel. Yet, unlike previous large-scale published series, the cultural legacy of the collected literature available via the Barnes & Noble's Nook, or Amazon's Kindle will be their 'empty' metal casings. Of e-books themselves there will be nothing. Ostensibly there never was anything. Yet to lament the lack of any physical object with which to judge the value of the e-book's cultural impact would be to ignore the fact that not having a physical presence is its *raison d'être*. Lack of substance – no bulk, no weight and its the contents presented in exactly the same way – was (and is) its celebrated Unique Selling Proposition.

When the first Kindle appeared in 2007, the American writer Jonathan Franzen, complaining of the vacuous reading experience offered by e-books, told the *LA Times*, '...the difference between [reading] Shakespeare on a BlackBerry and Shakespeare in the Arden Edition is like the difference between vows taken in a shoe store and vows taken in a cathedral,' adding, 'Am I fetishising ink and paper? Sure, and I'm fetishising truth and integrity too'.[110] Comments of this kind were not uncommon (the illustrator Maurice Sendak said of the e-book, 'It isn't another kind of book! A book is a book is a book'[111]) but were drowned out by the alternative, and far more news-worthy story usually titled 'The Printed Book is Dead'. But now that the sale of e-books has begun to fall away (by fourteen per cent in 2015 compared to the previous year[112]) the legacy of the e-book is becoming clear: a revivification of print. As if to emphasise this point, the most poignant paper-and-ink publishing success between 2015 and 2017 has been in children's books.

Books for children

Digital technology has exposed, better than any previous interloper, the sheer physical diversity of print. Nowhere is this better demonstrated than in books written and designed for young children. For today's pre-school child the digital screen, in all its forms, would seem to be the natural place to seek entertainment. The layered structure of material content on a tablet computer is mastered as easily as turning the pages of a book by young and unencumbered minds. In such circumstances, it was easy to assume that the colour, movement, music and sound effects – to say nothing of the empowerment that touchscreen 'buttons' offer small fingers – would prove too attractive for the printed book to compete with. In the words of Ted Nelson, electronic text's greatest proponent, 'the question is not *can*

Below:
Alphabet, designed and illustrated by Kvêta Pacovská, was originally published in Germany in 1992, this edition was published by the Tate Gallery, London, in 2012, and includes numerous examples of paper engineering as well as multiple printing techniques.

we do everything on screens, but *when* will we, [...] its simple obviousness defies argument'.[113] And yet, for young children, digital technology, like radio and television, is now settling comfortably into its rightful niche alongside the books on their shelves and the toys in their box.

Books for young children have particular problems to solve that involve far more than what is printed on its pages. The size and shape of a child's book is less constricted than more conventional books because their physical form is so much more important. A child can curl up and seemingly enter a larger book with friends or parents; a shared physical immersion encouraged by big pages saturated in rich colours and textures. Smaller, more intricately structured books offer a very different sensory experience requiring, perhaps, more dexterous handling. Such pages might be made of thick card and laminated to make them virtually indestructible, or of paper so thin that an image appears only when held up to a light. So many materials other than paper have been used to provide curiosity value including wood, foil, mirror card, string, leather, celluloid, woven materials, clear plastic etc.

The Czech illustrator, Kvêta Pacovská, born in 1928, specialised in 'object books':

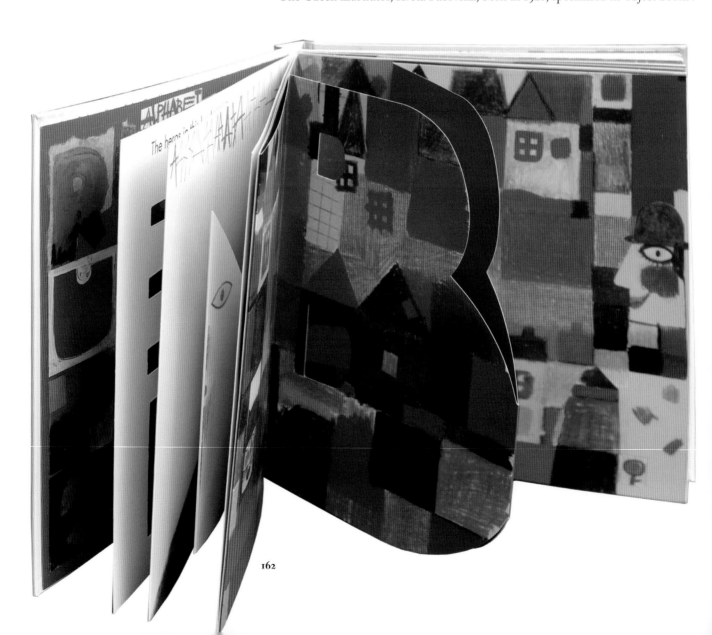

Below:
Kvêta Pacovská, paper sculpture/mask, c. 1990.

Below right:
The sales of books for young children has increased dramatically in recent years, enough to persuade major publishers, such as Thames & Hudson (illustrated here) and others, to produce a separate biannual catalogue to showcase their range of children's books. This cover is matt laminated with a textured spot varnish over the green. January 2017.

tactile, three-dimensional books with illustrations of stories for children that use a variety of materials and print finishes. Her books are often large and bulky – Pacovská preferring her books to be capable of standing by themselves[114] – and include curious collages, mirrors and superimpositions of different kinds of paper and cut-outs which, together with various print techniques, generate a powerful spell. This is achieved less by visualising the words but, instead, by providing 'a more total experience of the book as a means to link the spirit to the adventure of turning the page'.[115] Her illustrations are immediately recognisable for the use of bold, saturated colours presenting semi-abstract forms that are sometimes reminiscent of 20th century art movements. Her enthusiasm for geometric and abstract shapes is often based on the use of typographic letterforms, as in *Alphabet* in which letters and numbers merge with imagined creatures. One of her last works, *Unfold/Enfold* (2005) is a smaller format fold-out object book but capable of expanding to almost

twenty feet in length, and includes geometric die-cuts, unexpected pop-up elements, as well as her characteristic rich colours, squiggles, squares and quirky faces.

Pop-ups and die-cuts are just two of many transformational or 'metamorphic' features to be found in children's books along with folds, flaps and lattice interlays. Lattice novelties provide a change of image at the movement of a projecting tab – one picture appearing on one set of slats, a second on the other. Folds and flaps are less complicated, offering image change virtually at the touch of a finger. These features had been utilised in advertising novelties made popular in the 1880s and 1890s when chromolithographed folding cards showed split images of, for example, indigestion sufferers before and after taking a remedy, or 'bathing beauties' revealed *en deshabillé* in beach huts.

The field of advertising novelty owed much to the German illustrator, Lothar Meggendorfer, (1847–1925) who created and published a large and varied range of 'mechanical' children's books and board games using tabs, flaps, levers, three-part pictures, lattice interplay and every form of cut-out, animation and transformation including pop-ups within books. A natural progression of these mobile interactive

features were puzzles, games, optical illusions and 'magic', for example, 'magic painting' books in which colours appear when water is applied.

A child watching, for example, a character or animal rise from an enclosed space between the pages of a book achieves more than active animation. A popular page will be opened and closed repeatedly, first for the fascination of seeing the pop-up come to life, and then turning the page more slowly to control the action and inspect the paper engineering – cutting, folding, gluing – to try and understand how the movement has been achieved. That these physical mechanisms offer themselves up to investigation is over and above their intended influence upon the narrative and a bonus of the pop-up book. Unfortunately, inquisitiveness will sometimes be the cause of a complex mechanism to malfunction, and from which time will forever act as a reminder – and be a cause of regret – to the maturing child for earlier clumsiness. A child's book ages with its owner and the tell-tale marks and abrasions it receives serve as a pertinent record of the reader's metal and physical development. It is not surprising that parents find it impossible to discard such books.

Textbooks for students

Conventional wisdom suggests that current students in colleges and universities – 'digital natives' no less – would embrace e-textbook technology wholeheartedly. But results garnered from numerous recently undertaken research projects[116] suggest that this is not the case. Even more remarkable is the fact that this reluctance to use e-textbooks is despite the persuasive efforts of institute administrators to implement their use – not for educational benefit, of course, but to save money.[117] University libraries can achieve such savings by installing an access system that can be set to automatically disable availability when the end of a check-out period is reached and so reduce administration costs. In addition, e-books cannot be lost or damaged by students or, of course, mis-shelved.

E-book readers offer a number of genuinely helpful tools for study, such as highlighting, and annotating, (which can be removed) as well as an improved technology for note-taking or quoting. In addition, e-book texts are also searchable, allowing quick access to required names, places or key events. Of course, these functions are mimicking those activities that are, and always have been, integral to paper-and-ink textbooks. Nevertheless, the allure of new technology alone was expected to persuade the millennial student to embrace the 'paperless online classroom'.

Both Amazon and Apple have targeted the lucrative educational textbook market, running pilot projects (in 2008 and 2010) with selected universities using their devices as repositories for course content. To everyone's surprise, the trials generated disappointing results for Amazon, Apple and university administrators, with most students reiterating their preference for paper textbooks.[118] Importantly, and by default, the process of analysing and assessing the use of digital technology also highlighted those characteristics of print that enables it to work so well.

One of the main themes that emerged from these studies, and which has been a common thread throughout all previous research into reading behaviour,[119] is

Opposite page:
The reading room of the French National Library, Paris. There has been a dramatic increase in demand for such facilities since 2000. This is in spite of many major libraries now providing an 'on demand' document supply service digitally direct to the enquirer's computer. Easier online access to national library catalogues has helped to demystify institutions and their processes and encouraged readers to seek out the real thing.

that people read in a variety of ways, and students are no exception. For example, students might immerse themselves in a text, reading without interruption, whilst at other times merely flick through a text to get a general sense of its content or argument. Sometimes they search a text for a particular piece of information or a particular topic or they may jump back and forth between various sections of a text, to find comparisons. They will make notes, perhaps making marginal annotations, or highlight passages as they read. In other words, reading for study is a particularly idiosyncratic activity.

Books are exceptionally flexible as reading devices. It is easy to flick through the pages of a book, forward and backward, or to jump quickly between widely separated sections, marking a place with a thumb, pencil, post-it note or bus ticket. It is possible to write anywhere and in any form on any page of a book immediately, using pen, pencil or highlighter. Places of interest can be recorded for further investigation by turning over the corner or folding a page in half. In addition to supporting various methods of navigation, a printed book provides numerous subtle cues about the structure of their content that helps the reader to build a cognitive map of the book as it is read.

This extends to the individual books themselves and the physical relationship with each other. When a student becomes immersed in a given project this might be reflected and enhanced by the accumulation of numerous separate books which can be left open and spread out or piled on top of each other on a desk or across a floor to be dipped in and out of in order to collate related information.[120] When occupying a physical space in this way books provide gravitas to the project in hand and the reality of a looming deadline. But even when not actually being used the physical presence of books, lined up on a shelf or piled up on the floor, are a reminder of work to be done.

Below and opposite page:
Work in progress in the author's studio and
(opposite page) the opening pages of the finished
book: *Paris Perpendicular,* loosely bound and boxed,
with photographs by Virginie Litzler, printed and
bound by David Jury and co-designed by Litzler
and Jury, Colchester, UK, 2014.

Chapter 11:
The allure of making things

Skills and craftsmanship

Until the 1980s, most graphic design courses had a letterpress workshop, principally as an aid to the teaching of typography. Most of these facilities had been established by printing departments for their printing apprentices attending college on 'day-release' from their employers. When those apprentice schemes collapsed in the 1960s, the commercial printing machines and equipment were often inherited by the art school's graphic design department who were also, perhaps, able to retain some of the print staff to teach typography in conjunction with printing technology.

Their print-trade alliance had previously distanced members of the print department from the design process being cultivated by lecturers in the studio. For the young graphic design student, the printer offered a different kind of learning experience, a down to earth, rational, common-sense, even brusque attitude, and a total disdain for 'solutions' that did not take account of the practical limitations of the printer's tools and machinery. Their attitude was, 'if you want to use this equipment then use it properly, otherwise leave it alone'. Design lecturers, on the other hand, enthused about testing the limitations of this same technology and, by default, the printer's knowledge and craft skills.

Below:
An Albion Press, like so many today, occupied in a college printmaking workshop. This particular press was previously owned by a local newspaper printing company who used it for proofing before it was donated to Colchester School of Art.

This uneasy alliance had historic roots. The establishment of graphic design education in its own right during the 1950s coincided with the diminishment of printing courses, and it was obvious to all that this was no coincidence. The existence of graphic design courses formalised and gave credence to the notion that design for print was a quite separate profession from that of printing, which had its own set of values and skill sets. For printers and printing lecturers this felt like the end of a rich and heroic cultural heritage going back some 500 years.

Letterpress/typography workshops usually included one or more mechanised cylinder presses – usually a Wharfedale or Heidelberg – plus platen presses, a proofing press and numerous cases of metal and wood type. In an adjacent room there was often a monotype typesetting keyboard and caster, or similar. When printing lecturers retired the printing presses 'retired' with them. Mechanised cylinder presses are complex machines and an *old* cylinder press needs more knowledge than can ever be gleaned from its manual. Typesetting and casting equipment, renowned for their technical demands followed the same fate. It was

Below:
The complexity of commercial offset lithographic
printing machines meant that when the expertise to
run them in an educational environment retired or was
made redundant there was no one willing or able to
keep them functioning. Most higher volume printing
equipment was, therefore, discarded by colleges
during the 1960s and 70s.

disastrous that superbly engineered and sophisticated equipment was discarded
and, indeed, there were many design lecturers who mourned their passing. But if
there was no one with the knowledge to use or maintain them,[121] there was little
prospect of these machines ever being switched on again.

Without the rhythmic noise of large commercial presses or the acrid smell
of molten lead being caste, the letterpress – now more commonly called the
'typographic' – workshop, took on a more relaxed, even bohemian, aspect. Now
the responsibility of a design lecturer, the range of coloured inks dramatically
increased, as did the range of papers. Wood type, still cheap and plentiful, was
sought for its quirky characteristics and ease and speed of handling.

The shared point of contact was the proofing press. It was simple to maintain
and clean but, more importantly, it was remarkably easy to use and with the
addition of a guard to cover motorised rollers, also relatively safe. Wood type was
large enough to be inked up elsewhere using a hand-held roller, before bringing
it to the press. But the main advantage of the proofing press over automated
commercial presses, was that it was so forgiving of a student's attempt to hand-set
metal type. Instead of the type having to be secured in a metal frame – a time-
consuming task that had to be done with extreme accuracy if the entire setting was
not to become loose and crash to the floor – the type could be positioned directly
on the flat bed of the proofing press and, if speed was of the essence, even held in
place with magnets.

Despite their educational advantages, letterpress-based typographic workshops
dwindled in the 1970s. Phototypesetting was making its incongruous mark and
it was clear that major changes were afoot. By the end of the 1970s the rise and
influence of computers was already inevitable and it was clear that letterpress
was definitely, and very rapidly, becoming a redundant technology in commercial
printing. Some college administrators began to sense that maintaining letterpress
equipment, regardless of its obvious educational benefits, made them appear
ignorant of progress or fearful of change. Some merged their typography workshop
with printmaking. Others saw the political potential of the 'grand gesture' and
directly swapped heavy and space-consuming letterpress equipment for a dozen
desktop computers – 'out with the old, in with the new!'

At the height of these developments Alan Kitching was appointed, in 1992,
as a senior tutor at the Royal College of Art and invited to set up a letterpress
typographic workshop. It was a remarkable appointment considering that this was
when media speculation about 'the end of print' was at its zenith. Indeed, general
interest in print, as such, could not have been at a lower ebb.

Kitching, who had begun his career as a printing apprentice in the mid 1950s
at the age of 15, became aware of modern typographic design through magazines
such as *Printing Review* and *British Printer*, and discovered figures such as Jan
Tschichold, who influenced his early experimental work. But, more important, it
was while working as a print technician at Watford College of Technology, that
Kitching met typographer Anthony Froshaug who had arrived there as the new
Head of the Design School. Froshaug was unusual in that he had previously ran

Below:
Anthony Froshaug, both sides of a seasonal card, A6, the sparse use of red was deemed sufficiently celebratory for the purpose. ISO Standard paper sizes had only recently been adopted in Britain at this time. Printed 1961.

Opposite page, top:
Printing Review, number 58, 1952. This journal aimed to reflect the symbiotic relationship between graphic design and printing, with emphasis placed on cultural significance and creative potential.

Opposite page, bottom:
Alan Kitching, front and back cover of the *Prospectus* for courses he ran at his Typographic Workshop. Printed letterpress, London, 1992.

his own one-man commercial printing enterprise. Froshaug was a distinctly unorthodox modernist and Kitching was attracted by the unerring logic of his methods and the uncompromising – bordering on anarchic – nature of its making. Froshaug wanted to set up a stand-alone experimental type workshop within the Design School at Watford, and Kitching secured the post of running it.

Later, in 1977, Kitching set up the Omnific studio in Covent Garden, London, with graphic designers Martin Lee and Derek Birdsall who he had met through Anthony Froshaug and worked with when he took up a part-time teaching post at St Martin School of Art. When type foundries began selling off their stock Kitching bought a press and a quantity of type 'at knock-down prices' for Omnific and installed it at their new studio. Kitching continued designing and printing there for several more years before finally setting up a typography workshop of his own. When Birdsall later became Professor of Graphic Design at the Royal College of Art (replacing the Dutch graphic designer, Gert Dunbar in 1987) he persuaded Kitching to join him and teach (on a part-time basis) in the RCA's existing letterpress workshop. When the workshop came under threat from the new rector, Jocelyn Stevens, it was the students – with some encouragement from the staff – who forced Stevens to back down.[122]

It was the series of workshops organised by Kitching, alongside the unflappable print technician Mick Perry, that had caused such passionate support from the students. The results of these workshops (each limited to six students, two days a week for a three-week period and open to students from all disciplines) were seen

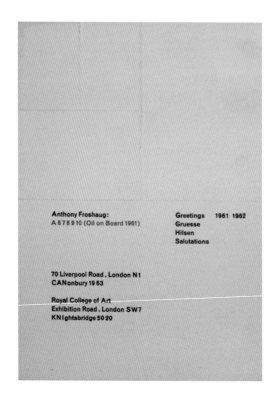

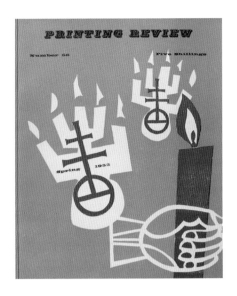

at the annual student Postgraduate Summer exhibitions, and so Kitching's workshops garnered international notoriety with astonishing speed. The creative potential of ink and paper with wood and metal type was quickly fed back into other colleges. Letterpress was not only re-evaluated, but reborn, this time as a 'new' and innovative post-digital technology: more immediate, versatile, adaptable, cheaper, recyclable and fun.

Almost identical political struggles to those experienced by Kitching at the RCA took place in most art colleges but the professional successes of Kitching's students and their subsequent sustained praise for the hands-on workshop environment they had experienced gave added impetus to the argument that the implicit knowledge gained by handling and moving real things around was a valuable counterbalance to that of the sedentary swivel chair and screen-based learning experienced in the computer suit.

The cause of type foundries cheaply selling their stocks of type during the 1970s was first phototypesetting and then digital technology. Small-scale letterpress printers, who had also been keenly watching developments, realised that they were being left behind by what appeared to be an unremitting line of new technologies massing on the horizon. Alan Kitching was not, by any means, the only person to recognise the potential of the letterpress materials that were being discarded.

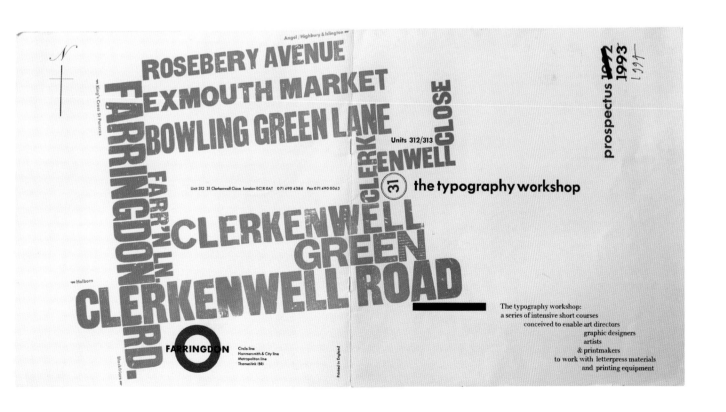

Below:
Fluxus artifacts presented as a cut-price mail-order catalogue. Fluxus newspaper number five, 1965. Printed lithography on newsprint.

Below right:
Page from a Fluxus prospectus, 1962. Design could often be essentially Modernist whilst also referencing the typography of the Russian Constructivists.

Opposite page:
Detail of an American advertisement c. 1950s. The influence of media, and of print technology in particular, on the communication of visual information was a key theme of Pop Art.

Print as a 'democratic multiple'

For some young writers during the 1960s, the rawness of stapled sheets of type-written texts or poems had been, in part, an expression of disdain for the authority represented by print. In particular, it was also a reaction to the pervasive presence, megalithic size and conservative preoccupations of the major publishing houses. But as the decade progressed the potential of letterpress printing, now a technology left far behind by the publishing establishment, began to obtain a vaguely radical or 'alternative' aspect, and so became an appropriate medium for the small, independently minded publisher to use.

Students who had attended art colleges and gained access to letterpress were not concerned, indeed were often not even aware, of its reputation for technical complexity. Technique followed vision rather than function and for most, letterpress was now simply an extension of printmaking while its potential for precision and craft-based subtlety was discovered later as needs required. The industrial (rather than fine art) heritage of letterpress print processes also changed attitudes and helped break down barriers. The possibility of creative independence meant that the fine art student no longer needed the compliance of an art gallery, and the graphic design student no longer needed the services of printer or publisher. The letterpress printing press was, once more – and in the midst of a digital revolution – offering not just new opportunities, but a sense of liberation.

This democratisation of print had a significant influence on virtually every aspect of cultural endeavour during the 1960s and 1970s. Pop Art's use of popular consumer products and especially its printed packaging became ubiquitous, with particular interest paid to the mechanical means of reproduction such as the varying size of the dots of ink in the making of a halftone or full-colour image, or the printer's trim and registration marks. And graphic designers followed suit. Fluxus was possibly the art movement that most enthusiastically utilised printed material to its cause.

Dick Higgins, the leading American Fluxus artist and publisher (who trained as a printer and later set up his own Something Else Press) believed that everyone was

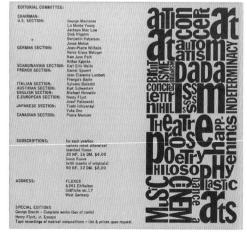

an artist – all that was needed was an outlet. Fluxus members aimed to demonstrate this by utilising the most elemental modes of expression including performance, readings and copious amounts of cheaply printed material – often in the style of printed ephemera: newsletters, tickets, sales catalogues, mailers, rubber stamps and the least sophisticated kinds of local advertising. Used in this way, incorporating photography, diagrams, text, drawings and always common, utilitarian typefaces, printing was considered to be the least pretentious, most democratic, versatile and accessible mode of communication. (Their debt to the avant garde movements some fifty years earlier was acknowledged.)

Higgins coined the term 'Intermedia'[123] to describe communication unfettered by media boundaries or conventions. In her book, *The Century of Artists' Books*, (1995) Johanna Drucker explained, 'Books [and other multi-leaved documents] were a form of intermedia par excellence, since they could contain images, texts and materials in a format that was flexible, mutable and variable in its potential to stretch from the sublime to the ridiculous, the ordinary to the unusual, the inconspicuously neutral to the absolutely outrageous – and to express personal, political, or abstract ideas.'[124]

Artists were, once more, turning to print as a means of avoiding what they perceived to be the elitism of the art 'establishment' in order to communicate directly with a general, rather than an art, world audience. But unlike the avant-gardists (see Chapter 1) printed matter in 1960s was a medium in which it was possible for the artist to have hands-on control if they so wished. The result was a period of innovation in which traditional fine art printing became inseparable from materials and processes previously exclusive to commercial applications.
Some private galleries encouraged inventive printed projects in an attempt to catch the democratic zeitgeist of the new independent artist-publishers. However, the term 'multiple', rather than the traditional 'edition' was introduced because it highlighted the unpredictability of the form such a book – or 'democratic multiple' – might take. The American artist, Ed Ruscha's *Twenty-six Gasoline Stations* of 1962, is an early example of an artists' book that perfectly fits the definition of 'democratic

Below:
Ed Ruscha, *Every Building on the Sunset Strip*, Los Angeles, 1966. The accordion-folded work, twenty-five feet in length, provides two continuous photographic views of the mile-and-a-half section of Sunset Strip one for each side of the thoroughfare.

Opposite page:
Much of Dieter Roth's prodigious output was in the form of books of various kinds, particularly journals. As a consequence viewing his work in exhibitions often tends to be limited to covers and bindings seen through glass cabinets (see also page 181).

multiple'. There were 400 copies printed, each consisting of twenty-four sheets, folded, sewn together, with twenty-six black-and-white photographs reproduced, each with a one-line caption. These books were made at minimal cost, enabling Ruscha to offer them to people who would not usually consider buying art from an art gallery. Variations on the same theme followed.

Ruscha used print as camouflage, presenting artistic intent within an object so common as to appear banal – the kind of banality that only a conventional 'commercially printed' document could obtain. (Ruscha had trained as a graphic designer and had worked on page layouts of the first issues of the journal *Artforum*.) In contrast, from the 1950s, the books of German artist Dieter Roth demonstrably shocked by their extrovert physical presence. Turning one of Roth's pages is never an incidental experience and will inevitably draw attention to the nature of the book's construction, juxtaposition of pages and extraordinary materials often included. The use of unstable vendibles (for example, food sealed between plastic sheets) meant that the document would remain in a constant state of flux (Roth was an influence on the early pioneers of Fluxus and relished the fact that his name was pronounced 'Rot') and so an 'edition' could vary considerably even without his handmade individual interventions and additions.

Although earlier avant-garde artists experimented with books by questioning their conventions, they did not take those conventions – of print, page and construction, or authority and stability – as the *subject* of their book as Roth did. In fact, for Roth, who considered himself first and foremost a writer, the book was all that mattered: 'I make art only to support my habit, which is to write and publish books'.

THE SUNSET STRIP

The physical dilemma of books

Roth and Ruscha in their different ways are pioneers in the development of the concept of the artists' book having both established reputations through work that explored, in essence, what it is that makes a book 'a book'. Artists have, of course, been involved in producing books for centuries. Peter Paul Rubens, designed title pages in the 17th century and François Boucher in the 18th century allowed the use of his work to illustrate books. However, a book does not become an 'artists' book' simply because an artist is commissioned to design a title page or to provide its illustrations.

Artistic ambition was a motivation for many publishers who produced so-called 'deluxe books' toward the end of 19th century – most prominent being the limited editions produced for French bibliophiles such as Octave Uzanne (see page 14). These were richly designed and ornamented, printed with great care and celebrated as prime examples of Art Nouveau which swept across turn of the century Europe.

It was in the midst of this printed opulence that the Paris-based art dealer Ambroise Vollard also decided to become a publisher, realising that books were a means of expanding the market for the artists he represented. The artists whose work were commissioned for Vollard's *livres d'artistes* were among the foremost of 20th century art: Pierre Bonnard, Henri Matisse, Joan Miro, Max Ernst and Pablo Picasso, although the books were edited and art directed by Vollard himself. The artwork was printed by the best lithographic printers of the time, such as Blanchard and August Clot. (The letterpress printers who printed the texts were not credited.) But whilst it might be argued that Vollard's books remain books with art in them, the books of other important French publishers that followed, such as Éditions de la Siréne, Éditions du Carrefour, and Raison d'Etre, might be described as true 'artists' books'.

Below:
Max Ernst, *La femme 100 têtes*, published
by Editions du Carrefour, Paris, 1929.

Opposite page, left:
Fernand Léger, *La fin du monde*, published
by Éditions de la Siréne, 1919.

Opposite page, right:
Henri Matisse, *Apollinaire*, published by Raison
d'Etre, 1953. The bold, flat colors and crisp shapes
are the result of the decoupage technique (cutting
up pieces of colored paper) that Matisse discovered
in the 1940s.

Artists' books have been described as 'the quintessential 20th century art form'[125] and yet they are notoriously difficult to codify. This, in part, is due to the hybrid nature of making books – the varied mix of activities that cause the reader/viewer, by the turn of a page, to be made aware of what materials a book is made, how it has been constructed and printed – whilst, simultaneously, studying its content. This is quite a different experience from looking at art attached to a wall, often behind glass, and requiring no physical interaction. Indeed, physical interaction is strictly forbidden.

Despite the huge interest in the relationship of books and art, galleries have been reluctant to exhibit books because they are such unwieldy objects to display. The working of a book does not lend itself to display: pages need to be turned, preferably at a pace determined by the reader/viewer, an entirely impractical scenario where the integrity of the artwork – including, of course, its physical condition – cannot be compromised. Paper can be strong but is easily marked and if the binding is anything but standard it will be prone to damage. Books are, therefore, usually placed under glass-topped tables, leaving the curator with the problem of what to put on the walls.

Two recent examples demonstrate the gallery's dilemma. Recognising the validity and public interest in artists' books the Royal Academy in London began accepting a small number of Artists' books in 2010 to their famous annual open *Summer Art Exhibition*.[126] Each year, before the exhibition opens to the public, the

RA holds an exclusive pre-opening event called the 'Buying Day' which is reserved for the Gallery's buying patrons. On that day, the security glass protecting the books is removed and staff with white gloves stand-by to open and turn the pages of any book a 'guest' might want to see. After Buying Day, and for the next three months that the exhibition is open to the public, all books are kept permanently under glass. Almost one hundred per cent of artists' book sales are limited to Buying Day.

A second example involves an exhibition devoted entirely to 'art and the book'. When the Victoria & Albert Museum, London, staged *Blood on Paper: The Art of the Book* in 2008, the stated aim was to 'exhibit works by outstanding living artists, including Anselm Kiefer, that took the form of books'.[127] In this case, all the artists had established their reputations through work other than books: painting, sculpture, photography or other media, and although a few of the works took the form of a book most were primarily concerned with 'the allegorical idea of the book – the book as container, as order, as a sign and prompt for memories – works that echo the functions of books'.[128] In this way, the V&A avoided the practical problems of displaying books by including a large proportion of work that were not, in fact,

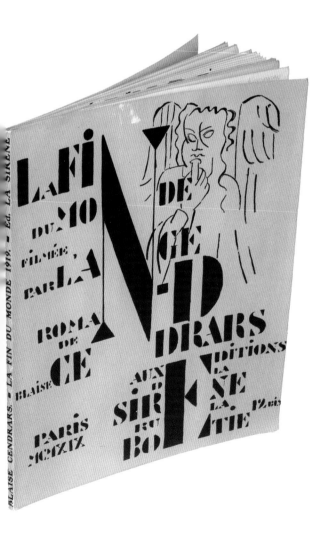

books at all, but sculpture about books. In this way the curators created an exhibition that fully occupied the allotted spaces with a range of objects hugely variant in size, volume and materials. The result made a fascinating exhibition, but it was not an exhibition concerning 'the art *of* the book'.

Printed matter as art

Frustrated by the lack of a forum or the means of showing or distributing printed
material, a group of artists in 1976, including Sol Le Witt and writer and art critic
Lucy Lippard, founded an art space (*not* an art gallery) in the Tribeca district of
New York City and called it Printed Matter. It was, in fact, part shop, part gallery,
and part publishing house, and the printed materials it aimed to encourage were
documents created solely by artists, not publishers. Taking Ruscha's *26 Gasoline
Stations* (rather than, for example, the more complex editions of Roth) emphasis
was placed on the democratic opportunities offered by print to provide the broadest
possible distribution of art. As a result, the works published and distributed by
Printed Matter were generally capable of being mass-produced in larger batches of
affordable editions. This is reflected in the utilitarian appearance of the website and
printed promotional material. An emphatic lack of pretension was also apparent
in the shop frontage – the very antithesis of the art gallery, preferring, instead, to
assimilate itself within the local community. (The new premises, a move forced onto
Printed Matter following flood damage,[129] has a jarring mock Edwardian frontage.)

The website explains what kind of publications Printed Matter will accept: 'We
are looking for artists' publications that are democratically available, inexpensive and
produced in large or open editions rather than limited editions or unique books.' The
most common prices of books on their website (July 2017) are between $10 and $15.

In 2006, Printed Matter organised its first NY Art Book Fair and this has
become a firm annual event. Locations have changed, often using major art gallery
spaces but during the last few years MOMA PS1 – an adjunct of the famous Museum
of Modern Art Gallery in Manhattan – has been the favoured location. Collaboration
with the acme of art galleries is excused by the fair's director, Shannon Michael
Cane, '…PS1 is one of my favorite museum spaces in New York City. But also, I like
the fact that it is a kind of a bastard child of MOMA.'[130]

The venue is large but Printed Matter is also not short of artists wanting a space.
The process of choosing who takes part is done in part by written application and
part by invitation. Most striking, however, are the huge visitor numbers – in 2015
around 36,000 over the three-day period. This has become one of its most distinctive
aspects, creating a huge, hot, crowded market place to which many of the 370
exhibitors respond by offering eye-candy in the form of badges, tote bags, greetings
cards and any other miscreant material that might cause the human flow to pause.

The successes of Printed Matter (it now also holds a fair in Los Angeles) has
had a profound influence on the way artists' books are perceived, so much so that
for many, artists' books are synonymous with cheapness. For some artists, this will
have been wholly intentional and appropriate – having embraced the elemental or
high volume commercial print processes and the cheapest papers in order to create
an impactful (though, perhaps, no less profound) statement. But for others, the
limitations imposed by Printed Matter: that a book must be an 'open' edition
(meaning it is capable of being mechanically reproduced to order, without any
intervention by the artist) is a severe impediment. When a point is reached in
which materials need to be less customary, when type must to be more precise,

Below:
Art Los Angeles Reader, a free 'newspaper' published for Printed Matter's Los Angeles Book Fair, 2014.

Below right:
Printed Matter's new shop and headquarters, New York, 2017. The policy of concentrating on cheaper, more accessible book art means that such works tend to be physically slight and therefore vulnerable, making them difficult to display and store.

colour more intense, and when it is necessary for a page to feel and move in a particular way when turned, artists will find themselves thinking about the necessity of closer affinity with the materials and how, precisely, they are made to work. In other words, 'craft'. It is creatively wretched and intellectually stunting to separate art and craft, but Printed Matter appear determined to do so.

With sophisticated digital processes woven into the very fabric of our society, craftsmanship can, indeed, seem redundant. And yet, this is the very point when those values of individual distinctiveness become most revered. For those in the maelstrom of creative industries, where distinctiveness remains so highly valued, craftsmanship remains a prized asset. And as craft skills and knowledge become more scarce, so their value increases.

But craft describes a process not an outcome, and anyone in the 21st century calling themselves an artist, graphic designer, printmaker, or typographer will share a broad range of working methods and processes as well as media. The dissolving of divisions (of which digital technology has played a major part) provides so many more creative opportunities in which craft has a part to play.

Print and craft: New creative possibilities

In contrast to book artists, the makers of 'fine press' books were often accused of relying *too much* on craft whilst showing little interest in the creative opportunities of print. The root of this perception reflects the initial modest intentions and the aversion of fine press practitioners to showmanship, or indeed, attention of any kind.

Beginning in the late 1960s with the closure of many small high-street printers, the availability of letterpress print technology – essentially unchanged for 450 years – was of great interest to bibliophiles, print historians, lovers of literature and book-shop proprietors who had dreamt of publishing their own books. The term 'fine press' was borrowed from the private press movement that followed in the wake of William Morris' Kelmscott Press.

The intention for many of these new press owners was simple: choose an author or poet (sometimes themselves, naturally) and then print and publish a book that befits the text. Most (but not all) were less interested in design, certainly as a separate activity from composition and printing, and more in publishing. Often with little or no art school experience, the aim was often to reflect the appearance of past books of repute and apply those same characteristics to the job in hand. (The combination of a letterpress printing press and Monotype type is an excellent teacher of typography.) But freedom was the prime objective, the freedom to publish what and when they wished and in a form of their choosing without being answerable to anyone else.

However, any sense of nostalgia that might be associated with these activities could be mistaken. There was often a stern idealism that rejected the fascination for

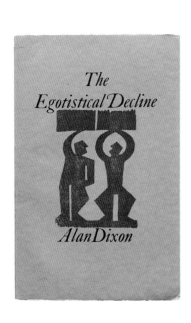

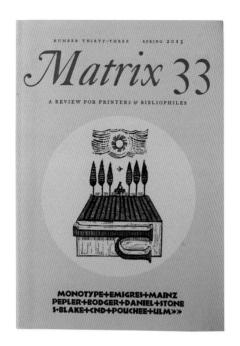

the fleeting, noisy, and multifaceted nature of communication that was dominating the consumer-driven 1960s and 1970s. The slower, contemplative process of fine press work, together with its interest in re-establishing recognisable standards of craftsmanship, was violently at odds with the economies of scale, speed and predictable outcomes of commercial publishing. John Randle's Whittington Press and his journal of book-like proportions, *Matrix* (published annually since 1981 and subtitled *A Review for Printers and Bibliophiles*) led and swathed a small but significant group in the UK before finding like-minded presses in the USA and Europe. For Randle, the purpose of the committed, independent, fine press printer-publisher was, foremost, the preservation of words. It is simply a coincidental fact that good printing onto good paper soundly bound – activities Randle is also passionate about – preserves words more surely (and surely more beautifully) than any other medium.

Whilst *Matrix* continues to be created in a quiet recess of rural England, another but very different journal, *Fine Print*, was the product of a distinctive and bustling urban environment. Established by its editor and publisher Sandra Kirshenbaum in the centre of San Francisco, it aimed to reflect a passion for diversity for which the city itself is so famous. Subtitled *A Newsletter for the Arts of the Book*[131] the first issue was published in 1975 and continued until 1990.

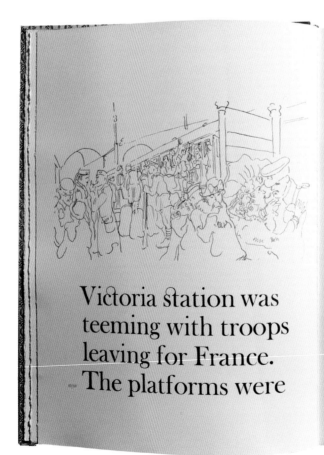

From the outset, Kirshenbaum sought to ensure the journal was free of parochialism. This is significant because California was already renowned as a pre-eminent centre of fine printing in the United States. Printer-typographers with aesthetic sensibilities, such as Edwin and Robert Grabhorn's Arion Press; John Henry Nash; Saul and Lillian Marks's Plantin Press; Ward Ritchie and many others, had thrived there during the previous 125 years. California's reputation was then rejuvenated in the 1970s and early 1980s when a veritable 'book arts revival' took place with the arrival of new presses, many founded by women: Felicia Rice's Moving Parts Press; Carolee Campbell's Ninja Press; Susan King's Paradise Press among others. These were initially established in the 'fine press', mould – meaning materials and processes were rarely less than perfect – but put to a purpose that was more spirited and often unconventional.

The state also has major fine press book collections such as Stanford University Libraries and The Bancroft Library as well as a major commissioner of fine press work, The Book Club of California, in San Francisco. So Kirshenbaum's policy, to seek a broader international view rather than fall back on the rich Californian printing heritage, was a bold one. Perhaps even more surprising, inclusivity also applied to technology, Kirshenbaum's view being that if it were possible that digital tools could help enhance or refine a hand-craft process then it should be explored.

Opposite page, top:
Matrix, number 33, 2015, an ambitious annual journal of book-like proportions, first published in 1981. Edited by John and Rosalind Randle, and printed letterpress by Patrick Randle at The Whittington Press. *Matrix* has focused on the book arts of the twentieth century, and is, at the very least, on a par with the remarkable seven-volume *Fleuron* issued in the 1920s.

Opposite page, left:
Miscellany of Type, edited, designed, printed and published by John Randle at The Whittington Press, Gloucestershire, UK, 1990. This book provides a display of all the types, in all styles and sizes, owned by the Whittington Press at that time.

Above:
Fine Print, edited by Sandra Kirshenbaum in San Francisco, and published quarterly. Kirshenbaum founded *Fine Print* in 1975 and was also a founder of the Colophon Club of San Francisco. This issue dated January 1987.

Right:
Carolee Campbell, Ninja Press, *The Intimate Stranger*. The book comprises of one long single poem, with each paragraph given its own page or spread. California, 2006.

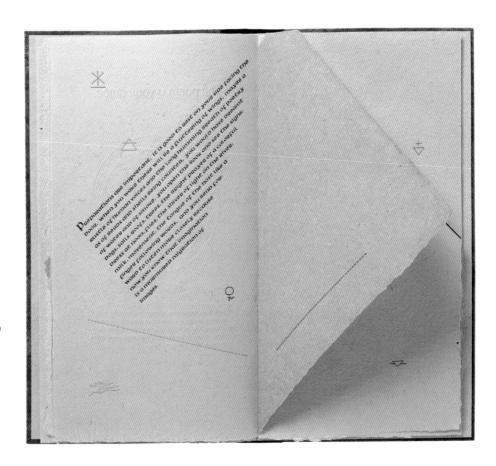

Below:
Felicia Rice, Moving Parts Press, *Codex Espangliensis: From Columbus to the Border Patrol.* The artist is Enrique Chagoya, author Guillermo Gómez-Peña. The book, letterpress printed from photopolymer plates, extends to thirty-two feet in length, California, 1998.

Opposite page, top:
Ron King, Circle Press, *Anansi Company,* a boxed set of sheets holding movable wire and paper puppets, designed and silkscreen printed by King in close collaboration with the poet Roy Fisher, London, 1992.

Opposite page, bottom:
Sam Winston, *Orphan,* 2010. Text set in multiple typefaces and hand lettering. Digitally printed with pigment ink onto 28gsm translusent paper. Winston, with Karen Bleitz and Victoria Bean, established Arc Editions in 2007 at the invitation of Ron King as an extension of his Circle Press.

Fine Print offered an optimistic view of craft, technology and, importantly, a future in which printing gave fine press practitioners license to move away from celebrated past norms and, instead, seek out innovative use of tools and materials. She was not alone of course, the Californian fine presses all aimed to take fine press into uncharted territory without compromising craftsmanship.

In the UK, and at about same time, Ron King's Circle Press was established. Having initially worked as a graphic designer, King was astonished and inspired when he saw Matisse's screen-printed book *Jazz,* exhibited at the V&A, and set up his press in central London in 1967 using silkscreen printing and, initially, commissioning a local letterpress printer to print any necessary texts. The difficulty and lack of success in trying to sell his books in the UK drove him to the USA where he gained the backing and encouragement he needed from academic institutions, libraries and private collectors to continue making books.[132] Most celebrated of these are King's nine experimental books produced in collaboration with the poet Roy Fisher. Paper engineering resulted in moving parts, wax was used to make paper translucent, and puppet-like characters on metal wire encouraged the reader to become a player in the narrative.[133]

Where there had once been an apparent irreconcilable gulf in both purpose and outcome between the book artist and the fine press printer there was, during the 1990s, a growing overlap between craftsmanship and creative ambition. This was also the decade when book fairs began to encourage the work of fine presses and book

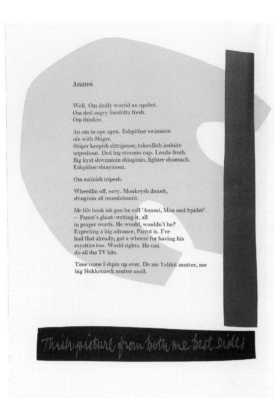

Anansi

Well. Om dedly worrid an upshet.
Om ded ungry forabitta fresh.
Om thinkin.

An om in ope agen. Eshpither swiminin
ole with Shiger.
Shiger keepish shtripeson, takeullish inshide
tripeshout. Ded big steamin eap. Loada fresh.
Big kyat shwiminin shlopinin, lighter shomuch.
Eshpither shtayinout.

Om eatinish tripesh.

Wheedlin off, eavy. Monkeysh doneit,
shinginin all roundaboutit.

Me life book ish gon be call 'Anansi, Man and Spider'.
– Parrot's ghost-writing it, all
in proper words. He would, wouldn't he?
Expecting a big advance, Parrot is. I've
had that already; got a wheeze for having his
royalties too. World rights. He can
do all the TV bits.

Time come I shpin up over. Do me Yabbit mutter, me
big Shikkenawk mutter anail.

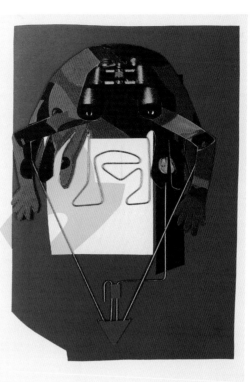

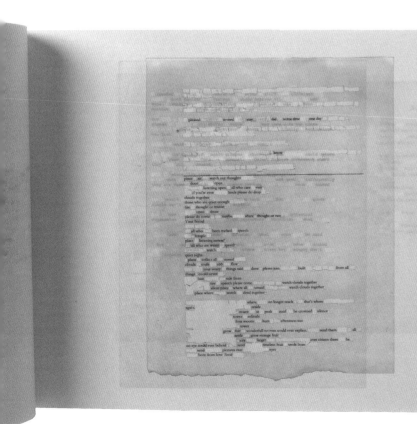

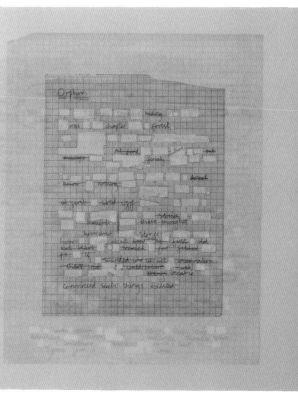

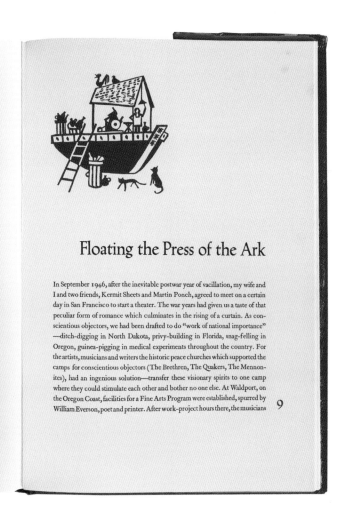

Floating the Press of the Ark

In September 1946, after the inevitable postwar year of vacillation, my wife and I and two friends, Kermit Sheets and Martin Ponch, agreed to meet on a certain day in San Francisco to start a theater. The war years had given us a taste of that peculiar form of romance which culminates in the rising of a curtain. As conscientious objectors, we had been drafted to do "work of national importance" —ditch-digging in North Dakota, privy-building in Florida, snag-felling in Oregon, guinea-pigging in medical experiments throughout the country. For the artists, musicians and writers the historic peace churches which supported the camps for conscientious objectors (The Brethren, The Quakers, The Mennonites), had an ingenious solution—transfer these visionary spirits to one camp where they could stimulate each other and bother no one else. At Waldport, on the Oregon Coast, facilities for a Fine Arts Program were established, spurred by William Everson, poet and printer. After work-project hours there, the musicians

9

Above:
Adrian Wilson, author, printer and designer, *Printing for Theater,* illustration by Nuiko Haramaki, California, 1957.

Above right:
Jack Stauffacher, cover, *The Journal of Typographic Research,* (later re-titled *Visual Language*) published by The Press of Western Reserve University, Cleveland, Ohio, 1968.

artists to be exhibited side by side. It is clear from their titles that the organisers of, for example, the annual London Artists' Book Fair (LAB) in London, and the biannual Oxford Fine Press Book Fair that both initially had one group in mind but found it advantageous to include the other, and in the cultural mix, inevitable comparisons and constructive discussions had a positive effect on all concerned.

The book art object

The changing function and broadening purpose of fine print during the past fifty years can be encapsulated by describing the preoccupations of Peter Koch, who became involved with printing in 1974 when, as a young writer in Missoula, Montana, USA, he founded the *Montana Gothic: A Journal of Poetry, Literature & Graphics* and a letterpress printing workshop called the Black Stone Press in which to print it. Koch taught himself how to print, referring to Clifford Burke's *Printing It*, a manifesto on self-publishing, and by the close study of *The Design of Books*, by Burke's mentor, Adrian Wilson. Everything else was learnt by trial and error on a treadle-operated, Chandler and Price 8 x 12 jobbing press.

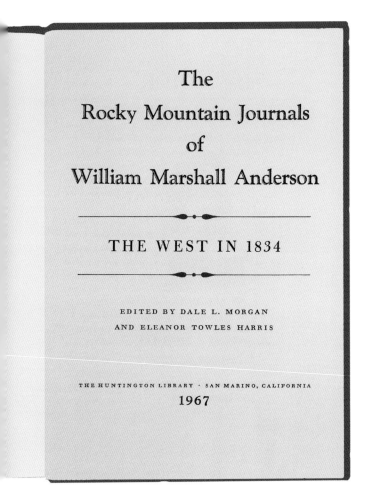

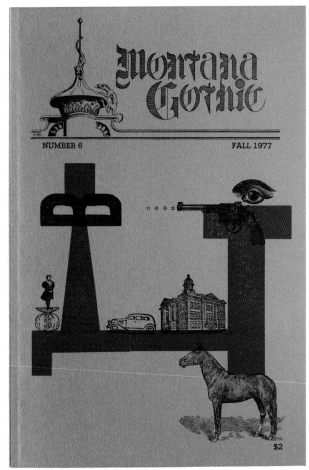

Above:
Ward Ritchie, designer and printer, *The Rocky Mountain Journals of William Marshall Anderson*, edited by Dale L Morgan and Eleanor Towles Harris, published by the Huntington Library, San Morino, California, 1967.

Above right:
Shelley Hoyt-Koch, cover designer and printer, *Montana Gothic* the sixth and final issue, edited by Peter Koch, Missoula, Montana, 1977.

Koch relocated to San Francisco in 1978 at the height of the book arts revival there. He now considered himself to be as much a printer as a writer, had already discovered the work of Californian typographer-printers William Everson, Warde Ritchie, Jack Stauffacher and Adrian Wilson, and wanted to learn more. In 1979 he embarked on a one-year apprenticeship with Adrian Wilson at The Press in Tuscany Alley and, in the years following, printed anything that helped pay his studio rent, from jobbing material – stationery, posters etc – to fine press commissions from the Book Club of California. Meanwhile, Koch was developing his own projects, whose themes led him to explore very different materials requiring innovative as well as traditional craftsmanship.

The high levels of exactitude sought by Koch in pursuit of creative accord is a characteristic he shares with the Californian book arts revivalists. Koch uses the term, 'fine press artist books', to describe their mix of 'renegade temperament' aligned with craftsmanship. 'High craft – high concept' defines work that tests standard craft practice in the pursuit of idiosyncratic ideas requiring discreet processes.

With the intention of providing an international focal point for what he saw developing around him Koch recruited like-minded fine press book artists to the

Below:
Peter Koch, cover of *Lost Journals of Sacajewea,* 2014, the binding incorporates bullets and beads (see also page 193).

Below right:
Peter Koch, two examples from an ongoing series of monographs collectively titled *Code-X.* Modest and beautifuly printed, simply bound booklets containing unorthodox and outspoken ideas concerning books, print and typography.

cause and in 2007 the Codex Foundation held its first biannual international book fair and symposium.[134] Here, the variety of forms that a bound paper document might take are prodigious, and the sense that print is being reinvented constant.

The creative renaissance of fine press work has had ramifications across a broad spectrum of book designers and publishers. Major publishers began publishing special limited edition versions of selected books (Thames & Hudson's 'Collectors' Editions', Phaidon's 'Luxury Editions', Taschen's 'Sumo' Editions, for example) in recognition of the renewed interest in the sheer beauty and public interest in the exclusivity of print. At the same time, the London Art Book Fair (LAB) held at the Whitechapel Gallery, invited some of the more ambitious, independent-minded 'mainstream' publishers to use the opportunity to display their less conventional projects and more adventurous design solutions next to the inevitable eclectic mix of books and other printed materials on show by artists, graphic designers, typographers and fine press printer/publishers.

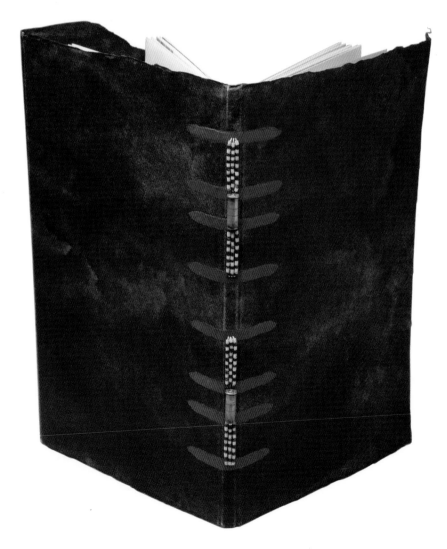

Below:
Henri Matisse, *Jazz*, a full-scale facsimile edition published by Thames & Hudson in 2013 on display under glass in the bookshop of the Tate Modern art gallery, London, 2016. *Jazz*, is one of the pre-eminent artists' books in the history of modern art.

Below right:
A2/SW/HK (Scott Williams and Henrik Kubel). Three of a larger series of books by the Austro-Hungarian novelist and essayist Joseph Roth, published by Granta Books, London, and designed (incorporating a bespoke typeface, *Italian Sans*) by A2/SW/HK, 2013. Launched in 1989, Granta Books is one of the many independently-minded, prestigious literary publishers to have emerged in the post-digital era and for whom high quality materials and design play a crucial role.

Post digital

At the beginning of the 20th century, the presence and popularity of the private press movement and the wave of 'deluxe' books aligned with Art Nouveau were, in their very different ways, a celebration of printing at a point when its future existence was threatened by a series of extraordinary communication technologies incorporating the telephone, film and the audio-recorder. The predicted 'electronic book' (page 13) and desk-top 'picture phone' (page 74) would not become reality for many more years. But when they did, reports of the imminent 'death of print' this time had a far more credible ring because the alternatives – in the form of the personal computer, smart phone and electronic reader – were no longer imaginary futuristic musings. 'New media' represented a revolution in communications technology at least as significant as Gutenberg's invention of printing from moveable type (which, it should be remembered, decimated the thousands of scriptoriums where handwritten books had, until then, been produced) and yet, some thirty years after the arrival of the Apple Macintosh, the authority and allure of ink on paper has not only survived but been enhanced. Re-emerging from the convulsions of a digital revolution, print media has recovered its *raison d'etre* whilst the authentic impact of digital technology has been its ability to lubricate the workflow and operating systems of page make-up and print production.[135]

Opposite page:
Peter Koch in his printing studio in Berkeley, California, 2014. The printed sheets hung up to dry are pages from *Lost Journals of Sacajewea* (cover on page 190).

The transference of raw text, image and artwork files across the world has provided huge financial benefits for publishers and streamlined the artwork to press process for printing companies whilst on-line book stores keep their backlist in public view. In all these ways, digital technology makes shorter-run book projects more likely by encouraging even the larger publishers to take a braver attitude to more effortful subject matter by turning shorter-run proposals into profitable propositions. The cultural impact (be it popular or more circumspect) of the major publishing companies remains, therefore, significant.

But there are many smaller independent publishers, indeed many thousands, who seek to remain modest in size and, by extension, focused on more rarefied, certainly more personal projects. For these smaller studios and workshops, the internet has proved to be a huge ally, whilst digital software has provided creative as well a cost-effective opportunities via computer-generated and processed artwork alongside traditional analogue processes. There is a genuine sense that whilst creators of print media have been able to recruit digital technology to serve its cause, digital technology appears fated to remain behind the screen.

Below:

Graphic Thought Facility (GTF). Cover for the *Royal College of Art Prospectus 1998–99*, London. With the use of digital technology already pervasive, GTF (then recent graduates of the college) chose to highlight elemental working methods and technical aids, in particular the photocopier, and demonstrate the process of design by the inclusion of paper markers, hand-written notes and instructions.

Below right:

Double Dagger is edited, designed, printed and published by Patrick Randle (Nomad Letterpress) and Nick Loaring (The Print Project). It is printed by both at the Whittington Press. The journal is of broadsheet dimensions and printed letterpress. The large letters on this spread were traced from laser-cut plexiglass and cut by pantograph into pear wood, 2016.

Postscript

The plastic has one big advantage: it is dead. It doesn't warp, even after many years. With wood you have no guarantee for this . . . but on the other hand we are unsure what happens to plastic in fifty years time.

The reinvention of print

Having almost reached the end of this book you are in the ideal place to pick it up and flick swiftly backwards through its pages. If you do this you will see that there are some page clusters almost bereft of visual material. These 'gaps' mark those pages on which digital technology is the topic.

The digital revolution has been truly remarkable in the way so many aspects of social life have been enveloped by its speed and ubiquitous presence. Yet, when looking back over the last forty-five years for visual evidence of this phenomenon there is very little that can actually be grasped. Even today, when screens display images and text of exceptional sophistication, digital technology resists its achievements being adequately recorded by other media. 'Other media' because the developers and manufacturers of both digital hard- and software appear to have little or no interest in enabling the recording of its progress or achievements. The resolute necessity to upgrade means that material evidence is lost as quickly as the new material is created. Digital technology deals well with the here and now, but leaves very little in its wake for us to savour, or even celebrate, because it consumes itself as it moves forward.

When printed material from the previous 650 years is studied it is, understandably, that of books, so often a coveted possession and created with their own substantive covers, which have survived best. But, surprisingly, we are also able to look at the ephemeral, everyday printed material that had a crucial role in enabling communities to function and, as such, carry all of the subtle social prejudices, transient tastes and incidental – and insightful – preoccupations of the time. Whilst national legal deposit libraries have the complex task of preserving material (both printed and digital) considered important by today's standards, the significance of transient documents and correspondence is impossible to predict and often not appreciated until decades, or even centuries later.

A written note can sit folded and untouched in a drawer for a hundred years but when discovered still be opened and read immediately. The same cannot be said of digital documents. With surprising candour, Vint Cerf, Google's vice-president said in 2015, 'We've been surprised by what we've learned from objects that have been preserved purely by happenstance that give us insights into an earlier civilisation', and called for the development of 'digital vellum' – software capable of providing

Opposite page:
Artwords Bookshop, Shoreditch, London. It is the 'bookishness' of books that shops now give priority, presenting volumes not only by displaying covers and spines but also fore-edges: *all* the distinctive characteristics unique to a book's physical form and function.

access to otherwise defunct digital files. Whilst print requires only eyes to be 'accessed', future scholars hoping to study much of today's culture will be faced with the prospect of deciphering PDFs, Word documents and a multitude of other file types that can currently only be interpreted with dedicated software and compatible hardware.[136] If a document is not printed the prospect of it ever being seen again fades quickly. It is a potential disaster that the responsibility for making and filing printed copies now falls to individuals and organisations who initially bought digital technology on the premise of a more efficient, space-saving 'paperless' work environment. As a result, an information 'black hole' awaits those seeking our initial steps into the digital world.

This might, in part, be the reason for the current resurgent interest in print, made all the more significant by the substantial fall in e-book sales.[137] That and the utterly miserable experience of on-screen reading. But it is likely down to more practical factors: firstly that the publishing industry simply discovered that all was not lost after all, shook itself out of its fear-induced stupor and began salvaging the full range of the printer's ancillary processes – foil blocking, debossing, die cutting, spot varnishes, laminates and experimentation with none-standard substrates, bindings and packaging, to reinvent the hugely variable physical presence of print.

As a result, the sensory effect on entering a bookshop is a revelation, especially for those having used an e-reader for any period of time. But it is not only their physical appearance. Picked up and opened, the reading experience is so much richer because printed books engage *all* of the senses. Each book provides a different and distinctive reading experience – even the act of turning pages again seems to make the reader more involved and, inevitably, more receptive to the author's words.

A book with pages that must be turned[138] remains a prized object. National libraries around the world do not support conservation programmes merely to protect a book's content – that will have already been recorded in a myriad of ways – but, instead, to maintain the integrity of the book itself and, in so doing, preserve those inextricable links with the place, the people and the time of its making. From the most lavish to the humblest and the most 'disposable', print has and will continue to provide invaluable cultural landmarks.

References

All web links accessed on 15 March, 2017.

Websites often have no page numbers or a named author or date. This, together with the fact that there can be no guarantee that the information, or even the website, still exists makes the point of offering them as a reference often futile. It is general practise, therefore, to include the date the information was accessed as an apology in advance – 'well, it *was* there, honest!'

1 Marshall McLuhan popularized the term 'global village' in *The Gutenberg Galaxy: The Making of Typographic Man* 1962 and *Understanding Media,*1964.
2 Peter Broks, *Understanding Popular Science*, page 39, Open University Press, 2006. Quoting a co-respondent in *Cassell's Saturday Journal*, 1898.
3 From a lecture titled 'Art and Socialism', delivered by William Morris to the Secular Society of Leicester, 23 January 1884.
4 Fiona MacCarthy, *William Morris: A Life for Our Time*, page 412, Faber & Faber, 1994.
5 *Pearson's Magazine*, March 1902 (London).
6 This first trans-Atlantic cable only worked for a brief period. It was not until 1866 that a durable telegraph link across the Atlantic was laid.
7 After being a member of the Société des Amis des Livres – which Uzanne found too conservative – he established two new bibliographic societies, the Société des Bibliophiles Contemporains (1889–1894) and the Societé des Bibliophiles Indépendants (1896–1901). Uzanne also edited two magazines, *Conseiller du bibliophile* (1876–1877) and *Les Miscellanées Bibliographiques* (1878–1880) and then ran three consecutive bibliophilic revues: *Le Livre: Bibliographie Moderne* (1880–1889), *Le Livre Moderne: Revue du Monde Littéraire et des Biblio-philes Contemporaines* (1890–1891), and *L'Art et l'Idée: Revue Contemporaine du Dilettantisme Littéraire et de la Curiosité* (1892–1893).
8 Octave Uzanne's article 'La Fin des Livres' ('The End of Books') was also included in the book *Contes pour les Bibliophiles* (Stories for Bibliophiles) published in 1895.
9 *Signalling Across Space Without Wires*, 1900, is the title of a book by Sir Oliver Lodge concerning the work of Heinrich Hertz (1857–1894) on radiowaves.
10 Before settling on 'Futurism,' Marinetti considered other possible terms, one of which was 'electricism'.
11 Vladimir Vladimirovich Mayakovsky (1893–1930) a Russian Soviet poet, playwright, poster designer, artist, and stage and film actor.
12 Peter Brooker, Sascha Bru, Andrew Thacker, Christian Weikopage (Editors), *The Oxford Critical and Cultural History of Modernist Magazines: Europe 1880–1940*, page 1,274. Oxford University Press, 2013.
13 O M Brik, 'Khudozhnik-proletarii', *Iskusstvo Kommuny*, no. 2, (15 December, 1918) trans. Lodder,

'The Press for a New Art', pages 78–79.
14 For example, El Lissitzky's *Pro dva kvadrata* (About Two Squares) a children's book designed in 1920 (and published two years later) was printed in Leipzig, Germany, by E Haberland and published in Berlin by Skythen in 1922.
15 'The term "joy in work" was conceived as a weapon in the struggle to reduce or eliminate the influence of Marxist ideas on members of the working class [...] to move the argument from work as a materialist practice to work as a spiritually satisfying experience.' Martin I Gaughan, *German Art 1907–1937: Modernism and Modernisation*, page 42, Peter Lang (publisher) 2007.
16 Key to this discussion was the architect Adolph Loos' lecture 'Ornament and Crime' in which he argued, 'Ornament is no longer the expression of our culture'. Why, he reasoned, would a society cover everything with unnecessary decoration unless it had something to hide? His conclusion was that the value placed on decoration was a symptom of moral degradation. See *Adolf Loos, Ornament and Crime: Selected Essays*, Riverside, CA: Ariadne Press, 1998.
17 It was the Bauhütten, the medieval mason's lodges 'in the golden age of the cathedrals' that inspired the name Bauhaus. Barry Bergdoll, Leah Dickerman (and others) *Bauhaus 1919–1933: Workshops for Modernity*, page 64, MoMA, New York, 2009.
18 When in London after fleeing Germany in 1933 Walter Gropius become a member of the Advisory Board of the Central School of Arts and Crafts.
19 Walter Gropius used the term 'new guild of craftsmen' in the pamphlet accompanying the Exhibition of Unknown Architects, 1919.
20 Stated by Gropius in a lecture given at the reception of the 'International Architecture Exhibition' organised by the Bauhaus in 1923.
21 Oskar Schlemmer in a statement accompanying the 1923 Bauhaus Exhibition described the aim of the Bauhaus being 'to build the Cathedral of Socialism', a reference that recalls Feininger's woodcut.
22 Le Corbusier, *Decorative Art of Today*, page 188, and written in protest at the *Decorative Arts* exhibition, Paris, 1925.
23 The idea of a simplified, single alphabet (replacing the combination of caps and lowercase) in which 'our letters lose nothing but rather become more legible, easier to learn, essentially more scientific' was discussed by the engineer Dr Walter Porstmann in his book *Sprache und Schrift, Verlag des Verins Deutscher Ingenieure*, 1920. Moholy-Nagy quoted Porstmann's proposals in his writings on typography during 1925. Capital letters were abolished at the Bau-haus in the same year.
24 Bayer's *Universal*, plus Josef Albers, Van der Leck and Van Doesburg's experimental typefaces have all been digitised by David Quay and Freda Sack of The Foundry, London. The original fonts were modified to improve functionality. See 'From Bauhaus to font house', *Eye*, no. 11, 1993.
25 'The printed surface, the infinity of books, must be transcended. THE ELECTRO-LIBRARY.' El Lissitzky, 'Topography of Typography', *Merz* No 4, (Editor Kurt Schwitters) June 1923.

26 Moholy-Nagy wished to protect the integrity of designing for print by keeping it separate from the print trade. '[When] creating an object becomes a speciality, and work becomes a trade, the process of education loses all vitality. There must be room for teaching basic ideas which keep human content alert and vital. [...] I can no longer keep up with the ever stronger tendency toward trade specialisation in the workshops.' Frank Whitfield (editor) *The Bauhaus: Masters and Students by Themselves*, page 254, Conran Octopus, 1992.

27 Renner took charge of a second school, the Munich Meisterschule in 1927 and it is this that is generally referred to when discussing Renner's teaching activity. Although quite distinct from each other in purpose: the Berufsschule trained apprentices for the trade; the Meisterschule gave a theoretical and practical education for those aspiring to manage printing establishments, a similar approach to teaching seems to have served both schools alike.

28 Johnston's 1906 book, *Writing and Illuminating and Lettering* was available in Germany due to Anna Simons, one of Johnston's pupils, translation.

29 The private presses in Germany were not perceived as being an alternative to the industrial printing maelstrom as in England, instead, they were seen as having an harmonious relationship in which ideas might be exchanged. Christopher Burke, *Paul Renner: The Art of Typography*, page 27, Hyphen Press, 1998. In fact, Carl Ernst Poeschel, Director of the major printing company Pöschel & Trepte (Liepzig) was also joint owner of the Janus private press with Walter Tiemann, type designer and Tschichold's tutor.

30 Ibid. page 61. Quoted from *Denkschrift über die Errichtung eines Buchdrukertechnikums in München*, pages 7–8, 1926.

31 Ibid. page 63.

32 Herbert Bayer, Isa Gropius and Walter Gropius (editors), *Bauhaus 1919–1928*, Allen & Unwin, 1939.

33 Charles Baudelaire's essay, 'The Painter of Modern Life', from *Baudelaire: Selected Writing on Art & Artists*, page 403, Cambridge University Press, 1972.

34 The Metropolitan Museum of Art, New York, introduction to the exhibition catalogue: *American Modern, 1925–1940: Design for a New Age*, May 2000–February 2001.

35 Steven Heller, 'Thoughts on Rand', *Print*, page 106, May–June 1997.

36 Garland's *First Things First* was revisited and republished by a group of new authors in the year 2000 and a third in 2014.

37 Ken Garland, interviewed by Anne Odling-Smee, *Eye* no. 66, 2007.

38 From correspondence between the author and Wolfgang Weingart, January–March 2017.

39 Wolfgang Weingart, interviewed by Yvonne Schwemer-Scheddin, *Eye* no. 4, 1991.

40 Ibid.

41 Peter Rea, 'Dan Friedman', *Eye*, no. 14, 1994.

42 Edison had licensed his stencil duplicating patents to A B Dick in 1887. Dick initially produced a flatbed machine, having also licensed Edison's name so he could call it the 'Edison Mimeograph'. Dick coined the word 'mimeograph' at that time, and the turn of the century saw the introduction of rotary machines. (In England Gestetner was doing the same thing.)

43 Ron Loewinsohn, 'Reviews After the (Mimiograph) Revolution', page 222, *TriQuarterly* no. 18, (Spring 1970).

44 The University of Wollongong has made the *OZ* archive available online: ro.uow.edu.au/ozlondon

45 Mark Perry, quoted in *Q Magazine*, April 2002.

46 Steve Jobs, from his June 2005 Stanford University commencement speech.

47 Quoted by Teal Triggs, *Fanzines*, page 172, Thames & Hudson, 2010, from *Secret Nerd Brigade* (accessed online by Triggs 29 April 2010).

48 Punched tape, as with punch cards, was a method of information transfer that had been pioneered by the textile industry for use with mechanized looms in the 1800s. The punched card was developed by Herman Hollerith in 1895 and used for the American census.

49 Emanuel Goldberg during the 1920s and 1930s was granted a series of patents for a machine that searched for a pattern of dots or letters across catalogue entries stored on microfilm.

50 'The Office of the Future', *Bloomberg Business Week*, 30 June 1975. (Author uncredited.)

51 Some of the code remains on Tim Berners-Lee's NeXT Computer in the CERN museum and has not been recovered due to the computer's status as an historical artifact.

52 Vannevar Bush, 'As We May Think', *The Atlantic*, July 1945. In this article Bush described his conception of the Memex, a machine that could implement what we now call hypertext. It appeared just before the atomic bombings of Hiroshima and Nagasaki and republished in the aftermath in an abridged version in September 1945. Through the use of Memex, Bush hoped to transform scientific efforts away from destruction and encourage a collective mutual understanding.

53 Amy Shapiro and Dale Niederhauser, Learning from Hypertext: Research Issues and Findings. http://www.aect.org/edtech/23.pdf

54 Paul Delany, George P Landow (editors) *Hypermedia and Literary Studies*, page 117, The MIT Press, 1994.

55 Robert Coover, 'Hyperfiction: Novels for the Computer', *New York Times Book Review*, front page, 29 August 1993.

56 Shel Kaphan, Jeff Bezos' former deputy, quoted by George Packer, 'Cheap Words: Amazon is good for customers. But is it good for books?' *New Yorker*, 17 February, 2014.

57 Quoted by Stacy Mitchell, 'The Bookstore After Borders: Protecting Creativity from Consolidation', *Yes! Magazine* http://www.yesmagazine.org/new-economy/the-bookstore-after-borders-protecting-creativity-from-consolidation

58 Quoted by Steven Levy, 'Reinventing the Book' *Newsweek*, 17 November 2007.

59 As described by Tom Dair, co-founder and president of Smart Design in 2010: http://gizmodo.com/5504896/there-was-another-ipad-20-year-ago

60 Flash was initially called FutureSplash. When Macromedia purchased FutureWave FutureSplash was renamed Macromedia Flash. Its current incarnation is as Adobe Flash.

61 'Irrational exuberance' was a phrase used in a speech by Alan Greenspan, Chairman of the Federal Reserve of the United States, on the 5th December 1996, when he warned that rational investing was replaced by momentum investing. The phrase was given additional piquancy by Robert Shiller, a Yale professor whose book *Irrational Exuberance*, published in 2000, predicting the collapse of the dot-com bubble.

62 This is called Search Engine Optimization (SEO). Google have an site specifically concerned with this subject including links to informative videos: http://static.googleusercontent.com/media/www.google.co.uk/en/uk/webmasters/docs/search-engine-optimization-starter-guide.pdf

63 Jennifer Kyrnin, *Perfection is Overrated – Web Design is Not Print Design*. http://webdesign.about.com/od/webdesigntutorials/a/aa061404.htm

64 Ricardo Bilton, *The Latest Web Publishing Design Trend: Mimic Print*, March 5, 2015, about the design of *Wired* magazine's website to match the redesign of the paper magazine in 2013. http://digiday.com/publishers/latest-web-publishing-design-trend-mimic-print

65 Abigail Sellen and Richard Harper, *The Myth of the Paperless Office*, page 8, MIT Press, 2002.

66 Ricardo Bilton, *The Latest Web Publishing Design Trend: Mimic Print*, March 5, 2015. http://digiday.com/publishers/latest-web-publishing-design-trend-mimic-print

67 *Emigre*, 'Starting from Zero' issue no. 19, 1991.

68 Found in 1907, the *Diamond Sūtra* had been hidden for centuries in a sealed-up cave in north-west China, and is currently the world's earliest complete survival of a dated printed book. Seven strips of yellow-stained paper were printed from carved wooden blocks and pasted together to form a scroll over five metres long. Although not the earliest example of a printed book, it is the oldest to be found bearing a date. The *Diamond Sūtra* is in the collection of the British Library.

69 The Library of Congress, Washington, acts as the legal deposit library for the USA.

70 Marshall McLuhan, *The Gutenberg Galaxy: The Making of Typographic Man*, page 279, Routledge & Kegan, 1962.

71 Lev Manovich, *The Language of New Media*, MIT Press, 2001.

72 https://en.wikipedia.org/wiki/Google_Books_Library_Project

73 In correspondence with the author, 2016. Anonymity requested.

74 British Library, *Digital Preservation Strategy*, page 5, March 2013.

75 The British Library has been collecting UK websites since 2004. (The UK web space contained approximately four million websites in 2013.) Annual 'snap shots' are collected to provide an historic perspective and to locate information no longer available on the live Web. Websites are collected with the permission of website owners. See: http://www.webarchive.org.uk/ukwa/

76 http://home.cern/topics/birth-web

77 http://first-website.web.cern.ch/blog/lmb-hack-days-mark-boulton

78 Ibid. See also The Internet Archive: archive.org a San Francisco-based non-profit digital library. Data is collected automatically by its 'web crawlers', Its web archive, the Wayback Machine, contains over 150 billion web captures.

79 As of 1st January 2016, GeoCities Japan is still online. Its member sites are still accessible, and it is still accepting new account registrations, However, services are only available in Japanese.

80 Hiroshi Ishii, '"The Last Farewell" Traces of Physical Presence', *Interactions*, July/August 1998.

81 Walter Benjamin, *The Work of Art in the Age of Mechanical Reproduction*, page 7, Penguin Books, 2008 (first published 1936).

82 Tom Whipple, reported in *The Times*, page 17, of scented candles seeking to 'improve your sterile ebook reading sessions'. One brand, Bibliophile, even claims to be refined enough to let people choose different kinds of books, from 'Old Books' to 'Oxford Library' and 'Trashy Romance Novel', 17 May 2016.

83 Quote attributed to Dave Farey, by Jane Lamacraft, 'Letraset: Rub-down Revolution', *Eye* no. 86, 2013.

84 Catherine Dixon, 'Freda Sack: Certainty through craft: a career in type design, from cutting to computing', *Codex* magazine no. 3, (Ed: Paul Shaw) 2013.

85 Adrian Frutiger (Ed: Heidrun Osterer, Philipp Stamm) *Adrian Frutiger Typefaces: the Complete Works*, page 80, Birkhäuser, 2008.

86 As described by Leo Maggs in 2012: http://www.mercerdesign.com/blog/the-true-story-about-westminster-the-font/

87 Dr. Peter Karow, Font Technology: Methods and Tools, page 74–75, Springer Verlag, 2012.

88 This, and variations of this term were used by Bauhaus tutors Wassily Kandinsky, László Moholy-Nagy and Josef Albers in an attempt to set out a universally understood vocabulary for visual communication.

89 Paolo Palma, *New Alphabet: Wim Crouwel e la tipografia sperimentale*, page 68, (publisher and date of publication not provided).

90 Jan Middendorp, *Dutch Type*, page 121, 010 (pub) 2004.

91 Interview with Jan Middendorp, MyFonts newsletter, no. 74, October 2013, http://www.myfonts.com/newsletters/cc/201310.html Bitstream donated a version of *Charter* to the X Consortium in 1992 allowing the font to be freely redistributed. *Charter Pro* was released in 2004 with an expanded character set.

92 Joseph Plambeck, *The New York Times*, 26 April 2010.

93 'The Future of Journalism', hearing before the Sub-committee on Communications, Technology, and the Internet, 6 May 2009: www.gpo.gov/fdsys/pkg/CHRG-111shrg52162/html

94 Neville Brody interviewed by Rick Poynor, *Eye*, no. 6, 1992.

95 Michèle-Anne Dauppe, 'Agents of Change Convene in Berlin', *Eye* no. 20, 1996. The theme of the Berlin Fuse conference was 'End of Print'.

96 Jon Wozencroft, Fuse 1–20: *From Invention to Antimatter: Twenty Years of Fuse*, page 7, Taschen, 2012.

97 Quoted by John O'Reilly, 'Visual journalism: Magazines and technology' *Eye*, no. 36, 2000.

98 Mark Hooper, 'Who says Print is Dead?' *The Guardian*, 3 June 2012.

99 The origin of this term may be the meeting of Neville Brody and David Carson for an interview for *Creative Review* (1994) during which Brody remarked that, for him, Carson's work represented 'the end of print'.

100 David Carson in correspondence with the author, February 2017.

101 Whilst the *Enciclopedia Universal Ilustrada Europeo-Americana* is the largest printed encyclo-pædia, the 18th century Chinese encyclopædia *Siku Quanshu*, is larger by far, although only seven hand-written copies were produced. It is, in fact, more a library than an encyclopædia (the title translates as 'Complete Library of the Four Treasuries') consisting of over 36,000 volumes, containing 2,300,300 pages, required 300 editors and approximately 4,000 scribes (or 'copyists'). Only four damaged copies survive.

102 Microsoft attempted to purchase rights to use of the text of the *Encyclopædia Britannica* and *World Book Encyclopedia* for its *Encarta* digital encyclopædia before, reluctantly, using under license the text of Funk & Wagnalls Encyclopedia for the first editions of their encyclopedia. This licensed text was gradually replaced over the following years with content Microsoft itself created. See: Randall E Stross, *The Microsoft Way: The Real Story of How the Company Outsmarts its Competition*, pages 81 and 91, Addison-Wesley, 1996.

103 Karen A Frenkel, '*Encyclopaedia Britannica* is dead. Long live *Encyclopaedia Britannica*', 15 March 2012, http://www.fastcompany.com/1824961/encyclopaedia-britannica-dead-long-live-encyclopaedia-britannica

104 https://en.wikipedia.org/wiki/Print_Wikipedia

105 David Jury, *Graphic Design Before Graphic Designers*, Thames & Hudson, 2012.

106 In correspondence with the author, August 2016.

107 Theresa Lynn Tinkle, George Bornstein (editors) *The Iconic Page in Manuscript, Print, and Digital Culture*, page 1, University of Michigan Press, 1998.

108 Walter Benjamin, *The Work of Art in the Age of Mechanical Reproduction*, page 7, Penguin Books, 2008 (first published 1936).

109 Eduard C Lindeman, New American Library advertisement flyer, 1951.

110 http://www.theguardian.com/books/2011/oct/02/maurice-sendak-interview

111 Ibid.

112 According to the Association of American Publishers, which collects data from nearly 1,200 publishers. Reported in *The Publisher's Weekly* by Jim Milliot: 'As E-book Sales Decline, Digital Fatigue Grows'. 17 June, 2016. http://www.publishersweekly.com/pw/by-topic/digital/retailing/article/70696-as-e-book-sales-decline-digital-fatigue-grows.html

113 Theodor H Nelson, Literary Machines, Mindful Press, published in 1980 followed by numerous further editions. As Nelson's book was distributed as a hypertext document there are no page numbers. However, this quote is located in chapter one: 'An Obvious Vision', under the heading, 'Tomorrow's World of Text on Screen'. The necessity of such a lengthy location description for this quote highlights a problem with hypertext. (Nelson coined the terms hypertext and hypermedia in 1963 and published them in 1965.)

114 Kvêta Pacovská interviewed by Wendy Coates-Smith, 'The Children's books of Kvêta Pacovská', *Line*, no. 2, page 95, published by the Department of Art and Design, Illustration Pathway, APU (now Anglia Ruskin University).

115 Ibid. page 85.

116 For example, University of Washington: Cara Giacomini, et al *Exploring eTextbooks at the University of Washington: What We Learned and What is Next*, UW Information Technology, August 2013. Also, Purdue University: Silas Marques, *E-Text books Usage by Students at Andrews University: A Study of Attitudes, Perceptions, and Behaviors*, 2012.

117 For example, in 2009 California was crippled by debt and facing a £15 billion gap in the state budget. The then-California Governor, Arnold Schwartzenegger, dismissed printed textbooks as outdated: 'Our kids get their information from the internet, downloaded onto their iPods, and in Twitter feeds to their cell phones, [...] Basically, kids are feeling as comfortable with their electronic devices as I was with my pencils and crayons. So why are California's school students still forced to lug around antiquated, heavy, expensive textbooks?' Many school administrators grasped the opportunity despite a lack of evidence to support Schwartzenegger's personal assumptions. http://news.sky.com/story/700287/schwarzenegger-termi-nates-school-textbooks 9 June, 2009.

118 Joanne McNeish, et al, 'The Surprising Foil to On-line Education: Why Students Won't Give Up Paper Textbooks', *Journal for Advancement of Marketing Education*, page 58, Vol. 20, no. 3, 2012.

119 For example, Miles A Tinker, *Legibility of Print*, Iowa State University Press, 1963.

120 Nicholas Carr blog, *Rough Type*: 'E-textbooks flunk an early test'. This one of several lucid blogs written by Carr criticising the imposition of e-textbooks on students for dubious reasons.

121 There were, of course, many who could, and would, be happy to maintain such equipment. The decision was one of funding priorities. Computers were expensive, staff needed specialist training. Meanwhile, letterpress printing presses were occupying space that could be converted into computer suites. The 'solution' was to make the print staff redundant.

122 Margaret Calvert interview (author uncredited) Calvert was appointed Head of Graphic Design at the RCA by Derek Birdsall when Kitching was senior tutor. http://www.rca.ac.uk/studying-at-the-rca/the-rca-experience/student-voices/rca-luminaries/margaret-calvert/

123 Dick Higgins, 'Intermedia', reprinted in *Leonardo*, vol. 34, no. 1, pages 49–54, 2001.

124 Johanna Drucker, *The Century of Artists' Books*, page 70, Granary Books, 1995.

125 Ibid. page 362.

126 Stephen Chambers, 'Artists at the RA', *Parenthesis* no. 20, 2011.

127 Dr. Rowan Watson (Senior Curator, National Art Library, V&A) 'Books and Artists', essay written in conjunction with the exhibition, *Blood on Paper: The Art of the Book*, 2008.

128 Ibid.

129 In 2012, Printed Matter lost more than 9,000 books during Hurricane Sandy. In October 2016, they relocated to a larger two-storey premises and includes a small gallery space, at 231 11th Avenue, New York.

130 http://www.ecadc.ee/fairs-masses-artist-books-and-politics-in-new-york-and-elswhere-interviewed-by-sandra-nuut/

131 The subtitle was quickly changed to *The Review for the Arts of the Book*.

132 Ron King, 'History and Collaboration: Circle Press', *Book Art Object 2*, page 78, David Jury and Peter Koch (co-editors) Codex Foundation, 2013.

133 *The Making of the Book: Roy Fisher, the Circle Press and the Poetics of Book Art*, http://onlinelibrary.wiley.com/doi/10.1111/j.1741-4113.2007.00476.x/abstract 18 July 2007.

134 For a record of exhibitor's work at Codex bi-annual book fairs see *Book Art Object*, 2009, and *Book Art Object 2*, 2013, both edited and designed by David Jury (*Book Art Object 2* co-edited with Peter Koch) published by the Codex Foundation, Berkeley.

135 John B Thompson, *Merchants of Culture: the Publishing Business in the Twenty-first Century*, page 321, Polity Press, Cambridge, 2010.

136 Vint Cerf warned the American Association for the Advancement of Science's annual meeting in 2015, that humanity faced a 'forgotten generation, or even a forgotten century' through what he described as 'bit rot', and called for the development of 'digital vellum' – software able to preserve old software and hardware – so that out-of-date files can be recovered regardless of age. However, more difficult still could be gaining the legal permissions required to copy and store software before it dies.

137 Ebook sales fell in the UK by 17% (The Publishers Association) and 11% in the USA (The American Association of Publishers) in 2016. Meanwhile, the total UK print book market rose 8% to a five-year high and in the USA sales rose by 3.3%.

138 Robert Bringhurst, *Why There Are Pages and Why They Must Turn*, Code-X no. 1, editor Peter Koch, 2008, The Codex Foundation.

Acknowledgements

The author would like to thank the following for their advice, knowledge, photographs, and/or access to their personal collections.

Andy Altmann
Sandro Berra
Chris Burke
Bill Burns
Chuck Byrne
Paul van Capelleveen
Steve Clay
Tony Cox
Oliver Clark
Mike Dempsey
Richard Doust
John Ellis
Len Friend
John Hall
Will Hill
Barry Hurd
Anthony Jury-Willis
Mikhail Karassik
Pete Kennedy
Peter Koch
Henrik Kubel
Virginie Litzler
Andreas Friberg Lundgren
Martin Salisbury
Richard Sheaff
Jack Stauffacher
Jeremy Tankard
Lee Thomas
David Wakefield
Brian Webb
Sam Winston

Picture credits

Index

Typefaces are listed together under 'Typefaces'. Similarly, magazines, journals and newspapers are listed under 'Magazines/journals' and 'Newspapers'.